Filipino
style

To Roderick,

Filipino Design & Style is our Proud
Cultural Heritage.

My best personal regards,

Mabuhay!

Rick R.
10 Feb. 2012

ARCHIPELAGO PRESS

is an imprint of

EDITIONS DIDIER MILLET
121 Telok Ayer St, #03-01. Singapore 068590
www.edmbooks.com

Project Manager	Elizabeth V. Reyes
Project Advisor	Doris Magsaysay Ho
Editorial Director	Timothy Auger
Editor	Jill A. Laidlaw
Photo Editor	Marie-Claude Millet
Designer	Joseph G. Reganit
Production Manager	Sin Kam Cheong
Public Relations Consultant	Henrietta Bolinao

This book was made possible through the generous sponsorship of the
Philippine Department of Tourism under Secretary Mina T. Gabor.

Contents pages: The gracious old Luneta Hotel, overlooking the Luneta Park by Manila Bay. Neo-Renaissance styles in the French manner with mansard roofs and grillwork were popular because of the local fondness for lace-like decoration.

Printed and bound in Singapore.

ISBN 978-981-4155-24-3

Filipino
style

Photographs by
LUCA INVERNIZZI TETTONI
TARA SOSROWARDOYO

With additional photography by

EMIL DAVOCOL

Main texts by
RENE JAVELLANA
FERNANDO NAKPIL ZIALCITA
ELIZABETH V. REYES

ARCHIPELAGO PRESS

Contents

Central Plaza, Vigan

A lovely twilight falls over Vigan in Ilocos Sur. Founded as a city in the Ilocos Region in the late sixteenth century on a high island surrounded by a river, Vigan has many streets lined with eighteenth-nineteenth century houses and is the best preserved heritage town in the country.

Previous pages: A grand all-white elite wedding reception at the nostalgic Ilustrado Restaurant at the El Amanecer Compound within Intramuros, Manila. Modern urbanites are evoking Filipino tradition by celebrating their weddings in Intramuros, the city's historic center.

An Island World

Fernando Nakpil Zialcita

aterials from a varied environment come together to form the Filipino visual style: timber of different strengths and colors from the forest; stone from ancient lava flows and coastal reefs; leaves and canes from tall grasses; and flat translucent shells from warm, shallow waters. In addition, Filipino style fuses together, in a unique manner, traditions from many continents: Southeast Asia, China (Asia), the Americas (Mexico, the USA) and Europe (particularly Spain).

This blending of different textures and traditions recalls the quintessential Filipino soup: *sinigang*. This clear soup combines vegetables, such as swamp cabbage or mustard leaves; onion slices; sometimes, taro cubes; and always chunks of either fish, pork, or beef. Its defining flavor, a slight sourness, comes from mashed green tamarinds, tomatoes, or guavas. The fine aroma gives a hint of fish sauce. At one level, the soup evokes ponds, farms, gardens, orchards. On another level it evokes continents. Soups made slightly sour with green tamarinds are found throughout Southeast Asia. So is fish sauce. On the other hand guavas and chilis came to the Philippines from Mexico, while our fondness for cooking with tomatoes suggests not only Spanish-American but also Mediterranean influences.

Until modern technologies created the temporary illusion that the environment could be ignored, architects paid attention to the precise configuration of wind, light, water and topography. A look at the geography of the Philippines is thus important to determine its influence on architecture.

Most countries are located on one of the immense continental land masses. The Philippines is an archipelago made up of many islands (over 7,000) and where the sea is a familiar presence in daily life. Three seas surround the Philippine Islands: the South China Sea, the Celebes Sea, and the vast Pacific Ocean. The islands vary in size and composition. Some islands are coral atolls peeping from blue waters. Other islands are large land masses that were spewed by volcanoes and are now watered by rivers running to the sea.

Mountains take up much of the island space, leaving little room for plains, except in Central Luzon and western Mindanao. River valleys are narrow and short. Some mountains are active volcanoes, for the Philippines sits on tectonic plates that press against each other as part of the Pacific Ocean's Ring of Fire. Earthquakes, of differing strengths, are thus frequent.

The Philippines, being in the tropics, are warm throughout most of the year. There are three seasons. From March to May the weather is dry and temperatures can soar to an intense, humid 31°C. In June, moist winds sail in from a different direction: from the southwest, from the Indian Ocean, bearing rain. By November, the rains peter out; dry cold winds from Siberia visit until February and can lower the temperature to 20°C. However, the temperature in the Cordillera Mountains of Luzon, where the summer capital, Baguio, is located, is uniformly temperate throughout the year, at a cool 19°C. Rain is abundant in most parts of the islands. Indeed, on the eastern seaboard, rainfall pours throughout the year. Typhoons are unwanted visitors—originating from the east, in the Pacific, between July and November, they race diagonally at more than 118 kilometers per hour, from southeast to northeast, causing destruction in eastern Visayas and Luzon.

Wood, grasses and seashells are favorite Philippine building materials. Where the dry season is short, dense rainforests grow and yield red and white Philippine mahogany. Other forests produce the molave which, when aged, can break a saw; and the narra which is fragrant and ranges in color from reddish-yellow to dark red. The pine stands of the Cordillera provide another fine wood. On the lower slopes of mountains and on flatlands, the vegetation changes from trees to palms and grasses. Some palms, such as the coconut, provide material for houseposts and thatch; others, such as the anahaw, the fan-shaped buri, and the swamp-dwelling nipa, are excellent for thatch. Rattan, a creeping palm, is used for bent furniture and for lashings. Among the grasses, the pliant bamboo can be used to construct almost all houseparts, including the roof. Thin-stemmed elephant grass makes good thatch. The warm seas

An exuberant mural portrays the Goddess of the Harvest being offered tribute by the folk-figures of Luzon, Visayas and Mindanao— representing the Philippines' three main island groups. The ceiling painting of this house in Malolos, Bulacan, was designed by the homeowner—to complement the four caryatids mounted on the house's façade.

encourage the growth of coral reefs along the coast. Shells like the beautiful capiz, are both edible and useful for interior decoration and building.

As in the rest of Southeast Asia, the earliest settlers of the Philippine islands were short, dark-skinned, curly-haired Negritos. They gathered wild plants for food in the abundant forests and hunted game. Around 3000 B.C., a new people crossed over from what is now Southern China to (modern-day) Taiwan, and then crossed over to the Philippine Archipelago spreading southwards until they reached the countries that are now known as Malaysia and Indonesia. These were the Austronesians from whom the majority of Filipinos are descended. As the southern branch of the Mongoloid family they are medium to tall in height, brown-skinned, and flat-haired. They became so dominant that even Negritos now speak only Austronesian languages.

In much of the Philippines, because of the low population density and the deep forest, the Austronesians practiced slash-and-burn cultivation, which opens temporary gardens, well into our century. As periodic shifts to other parts of the forest after two years or so were needed so that the unirrigated garden could be refertilized by the forest, large, densely populated centers, such as cities, would have been difficult to sustain. Only in some well-flooded areas, like the shores of Laguna de Bay, did people cultivate wet rice. Here, villages fortified with moats and towers were noted by the earliest

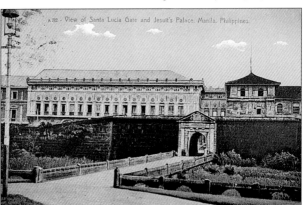

View of Santa Lucia Gate and Jesuit's Palace, Manila, Philippines.

Spanish explorers. The famous Ifugao rice terraces may well have been sculpted only during the past four centuries by peoples who retreated to the highlands to escape Spanish advances.

*A*nother disincentive to urbanism was at work. Until the end of the ninth century A.D., the Philippines was far from the main trade routes of the Southeast Asian region. The trade between China and India hugged the coastline of mainland Southeast Asia, while the traffic in spices took place between the Moluccas and the Malay Peninsula, passing through Java and Sumatra. In the areas touched by international trade routes people lived in compact settlements and practiced intensive agriculture. This way of living resulted in cities and stone temples.

But urbanizing factors did eventually appear in Mindanao and Sulu. By the tenth century, the kingdom of Champa (now southern Vietnam) claimed the Lord of Butuan, of northern Mindanao, as a vassal. The Lord of Butuan had much gold. Spectacular woven belts of gold unearthed in Butuan and dating from this time suggest the existence of a refined court with highly specialized artisans. However, when Arab traders began to frequent Sulu because of its pearls and rare bird's nests, Butuan lost its preeminence to Sulu. Jolo emerged as a city by the beginning of the fifteenth century. With the traders came Islam and mosques of timber and stone. Jolo became the nucleus of a seafaring sultanate.

Chinese traders came to Luzon and Sulu to exchange silks and porcelains for marine goods such as pearls, and forest products such as beeswax. Towards the end of the sixteenth century they settled in large numbers in Luzon and the Visayas. The Chinese wanted to trade with the newcomers: the Spaniards.

The pale-skinned strangers came in 1565 and made the islands the westernmost march of their empire. Christian missionaries gathered converts from their small settlements, into new centers "under the church bells." By propagating the plow and the use of the water buffalo as a draft animal, they persuaded the converts to switch to wet rice cultivation. Urban centers multiplied. They were laid out in grid pattern around a central plaza dominated by the church, the government building, and the houses of the leading citizens. Churches and other buildings constructed from stone appeared. Sculptors, silversmiths, painters and embroiderers used their skills to decorate these new structures.

A postcard from Intramuros (left), the Spanish walled city. On the remains of Rajah Solimaan's town, the Spaniards founded a city in 1571 and enclosed it with thick stone walls and a moat. Originally a protective enclosure for Spaniards, nineteenth century Intramuros became the home of many wealthy, native Filipinos. With its many ancient churches, schools and palaces, Intramuros was the heart of the archipelago until the bombs of 1945. Main picture: Within the same walls of Intramuros today stands the three-story Casa Manila house-museum. Constructed in 1981, the Casa Manila contains a fine collection of furniture from the Spanish colonial period.

Manila, now the capital, became the node of the first global trade network. Goods coming from other Asian countries, especially China, came to Manila, were shipped to Mexico (known at the time as New Spain) via galleons and then reexported to Europe. In exchange Mexican silver flooded the Orient. Through this trade, new arts from China and the Americas flowed into Manila. In return Filipino-made inlaid wooden furniture, cotton blankets, gold filigree necklaces and dainty ivory saints entered the Americas. Manila became synonymous in New Spain with a refined style of living. The town also gave its name to an exquisite silk shawl, the *manton de Manila*. Although many of these shawls were in fact embroidered in Guangzhou (formerly known as Canton), recent research has shown that some, along with other finely embroidered silk garments, were the products of Manila ateliers.

Still, the galleon trade never made the colony profitable. The hinterlands were neglected. Because of this, architecturally significant lay residences dating from the eighteenth century are rare. Instead the parish-convents were the largest buildings in town. Note though that, aside from being the priest's residence, they also housed schools which taught basic academic skills and useful trades; and they served as travelers' inns.

The economy improved only when the ports were opened in the nineteenth century and the hinterlands began exporting rice, abaca, sugar and coffee internationally. A native bourgeoisie flourished, sent their children to universities for education, and constructed substantial houses in the provinces. A vigorous, secular painterly tradition appeared. Painters such as Juan Luna and Felix Hidalgo went to Spain and France to train, won art competitions in Spain, and attracted a clientele. Some of the best Philippine paintings of the period are in Spanish collections. Architectural standards became stricter. Traditionally, builders were master masons and carpenters who had learned their craft through apprenticeship. Schools for arts and trades were now set up by the government; henceforth plans for new buildings were to be submitted to the government for approval. The government also imported Spanish engineer-architects. Significantly, they recommended building in "the system adopted locally" rather than originating European-style architecture, because the former withstood earthquakes better—as will be seen. Nonetheless engineer-architects brought over from the Spanish Peninsula noted in the middle of the nineteenth century how much more expensive it was to build in the Philippines than in Europe, primarily because wages were higher.

However, the Spaniards could not make up their minds about other aspects of policy. Although they initially liberalized the Philippines' trade with other countries, they eventually imposed import restrictions on goods from Britain thus encouraging Filipinos to buy goods and machinery from Spain even though these were more expensive than and inferior to equivalent British goods. While they opened a public school system in 1863, at the same time as on the Spanish Peninsula, and continued encouraging higher education for those who could afford it, they discriminated against locals in appointments to positions in the State and the Church. Meanwhile, the civil guards were arbitrary in their arrests, and even native government functionaries languished in prison for failures in tax collection. Peaceful reforms sought by national hero Jose Rizal and other intellectuals were eyed suspiciously. A revolution, led by Andres Bonifacio, exploded in 1896. As Asia's first democratic revolution, it sought to establish a republic on the basis of the freedom to speak, to assemble and to elect.

Leadership of the revolution passed on to General Emilio Aguinaldo who had won victories over the Spaniards. Taking advantage of Spain's weakness, the USA intervened in 1898. Although the Filipino army had won much of Luzon and the Visayas and had surrounded Manila, it was the Americans who took over the capital. In the war that broke out between the USA and the Philippine Republic, American technology won.

The new master pioneered in the new technology. Moreover, astute and democratic, the USA allowed Filipinos to elect their national leaders. The USA also invested heavily in public education, sanitation, and infrastructure. For instance, Daniel Burnham, the well-known city planner, was brought over to Manila from the USA to design a master plan for the capital. He gave Manila its Neoclassical government buildings and a new axis of broad, tree-lined avenues. At the same time talented Filipinos were given scholarships in design and architecture to American schools. The USA replaced Europe as the Filipino's role model in almost everything. Initially, the USA had no plans to concede independence. However, the Americans finally promised independence in order to safeguard their sugar and tobacco industry—cheap Philippine sugar and tobbacco was flooding the US market and undermining the profitability of these commodities in America. Despite the considerable disruption of World War II, the Americans fully recognized the Philippine Republic's sovereignty in 1946.

The Manila Hotel (below, left) was the social hub of Manila; while the colonial-style bungalow in Baguio (below, right) provided a summer respite from the heat of the city. It is Filipino-American domestic architecture that best displays style adaptations. The functional chalet house was a one-level, elevated structure with a wide porch.

A casualty of World War II was the walled city, Intramuros, where Manila had begun. Its many ancient churches and chapels, its beautiful palaces and residences were destroyed by American artillery and Japanese grenades in the fierce fighting of 1945. Only San Agustin Church and the city walls survived somewhat intact.

The independence years have been unstable, for it is difficult to run the ship of state for the first time, especially as a democracy with many problems. After World War II most Filipinos lived in rural areas where jobs, irrigation and roads were limited. The revolution did not resolve the question of large landholdings which benefitted the elite. The government had limited revenues to fund much-needed investment in infrastructue and education. Private armies proliferated in defiance of the central government. Moreover, in protest against injustices, two Communist rebellions and a Muslim separatist movement flared up.

But during these same years, industrialization began. Finally the Philippines was exporting more than just raw materials. In art, furniture, and house decoration, Filipinos established a solid international reputation. They confidently explored their varied local artistic traditions and reinterpreted these using contemporary designs. Meanwhile, local architectural schools produced talented architects who constructed modern office buildings and houses. In the suburbs of Manila, new towns were opened by developers which experimented with new ways of organizing urban space. The best example of this type of planning is Makati, Manila, whose postwar district segregates the high-rises of the commercial area from the bungalows and two-story houses of the residential areas and also integrates parks into its overall design.

Santa Maria Church

Its high and unusual location distinguishes Sta. Maria Church (built in 1824) in Ilocos Sur. A magnificent approach of 85 stone steps up a steep hill provided protection against pirate attacks from the coast, as well as a place of refuge when the surrounding plains were flooded. The church has thick brick walls bolstered by quadrangular buttresses—a style called "Earthquake Baroque". The solid brick façade is framed by two exaggerated columns; and a bell tower is situated near the middle of the nave. Sta. Maria Church has been chosen as a United Nations World Heritage Site, designated for preservation for future generations.

Philippine Forms

Rene Javellana

Filipinos love to embellish: houses, furniture, vehicles, clothes, knick knacks, anything and everything. *Horror vacui*, a term appropriated from Michel Touissant's characterization of Mexican colonial art has been used to describe the Philippine decorative arts—it means, quite literally, "the fear of empty spaces". This tendency is not uniquely Philippine; in fact, the Filipinos' love for elaboration finds resonance in the decorative arts of their Southeast Asian neighbors and in the Baroque style introduced by Spanish colonizers.

Nowhere are the decorative arts more evident than in domestic interiors. Not until after World War II did interior design find professional followers; and even then only very affluent homemakers employed decorators or designers. Guided by an unspoken sense of what is *maganda at tama* (beautiful and right), the town or city dwelling homemaker works with a range of choices when filling interiors. From homespun fabric, like the *abel* from the Ilocos and *hablon* from Iloilo, *sinamay* or *abaca* fabric, the gossamer *piña* woven from pineapple fibers, to cloth imported from Asia, Europe and the United States. From colonial furniture to the most modern pieces of plastic and stainless steel. From indigenous mats or *banig* to stuffed matresses. There is an excess of choice, a plethora of styles and materials to choose from.

Contemporary decorative arts were forged in the crucible of colonialism when a lively interchange between Western and Eastern traditions occurred. Building upon and redirecting traditional crafts to meet the needs of the colonists, introducing European and Mexican crafts, and encouraging the influx of Chinese goods, the two principal instruments of colonialism, Church and State, set the stage for the emergence of a *mestizo* or "mixed" culture. Under the tutelage of Catholic missionaries, both indigenous and Chinese carvers built elaborate *retablos* or altar pieces and church furniture such as pulpits and ceremonial chairs, which while European in plan used Oriental motifs. To augment the income of their parishioners and to finance their missions, missionaries introduced the frame loom, thus releasing women weavers from the restraints imposed by the back strap loom. Wider cloths appeared: canvas for sails and thick cotton for blankets, abaca textile for blouses, piña, and a variety of textiles that combined fibers, including Chinese silk. The state support of trade created, by the nineteenth century, a wealthy class who built large wood and stone colonial houses, the *bahay na bato at kahay*. In turn this created a flourishing market for furniture, which was almost absent in folk houses of thatch and bamboo (called *bahay kubo*). Silver brought by galleon from Mexico widened the repertoire of jewelers who aside from Church vessels made personal jewelry, silver services for the elaborate colonial table, key holders and candlesticks. The importation of iron from China and elsewhere made possible elaborate grill work, a constant element in colonial decoration.

The development of colonial furniture, kitchen implements and weaving demonstrates the fusion and adaptation characteristic of the colonial decorative tradition.

The indigenous *banggera*, a rack for drying utensils, remained a standard feature of colonial kitchen design. A cabinet with slatted bamboo doors for food and utensils, the *paminggalan*, was also a regular feature of the kitchen. The introduction of new recipies and their fusion with indigenous recipies called for the introduction of proper implements such as the coconut grater, and new implements such as decorative cookie molds.

Adaptation was also evident in the other rooms of the house. The bamboo bed or *papag* used in farm houses or by the household help was replaced by the *kama*, a wooden bed raised high with a woven rattan frame as a sleeping platform. The indigenous *dulang*, described by the chronicler Pedro Chirino in 1604 as a table "small, low, and round or square in shape" were built side by side with European-style dining tables, called in the vernacular *mesa* or *lamesa*. Eventually the lamesa replaced the dulang which was only found in farm or country homes. These tables of European design, some with Chinese touches like ball-and-claw feet, were built in a variety of forms. The *mesa altar*, as the name suggests displayed the family's wood and ivory *santos* or images of saints. Smaller or specialized tables like the *consolas* (side tables), *mesittas* (center tables), and *escritorios* (desks) were found in vestibules, living rooms, bedrooms and home offices.

Filipino style mixes art and artifacts, ornament and utility. The mesa altar is an exuberantly carved table. Here the table accentuates Simon Flores' classic portrait of the nineteenth century Filipina in her exquisitely embroidered costume.

For storage, the sea chest used by travelers became known as the wooded chest or *baul*. Large cabinets or *aparador* with one or two doors stored clothes, plates and books. A variety of chairs were also built; two distinctive colonial chairs are the *butaca* or *sillon* (planter's chair) and the *gallinera*. The former was a wide chair with a reclining back, a variation with wide arms was called *silla peresoza* (lazy chair), ideal for afternoon naps.

Eventually regional furniture styles emerged: the furniture of Ilocos and Bohol emphasized solid forms. The Batangas style showed a marked Chinese influence, Pampanga favored heavy Baroque ornamentation, while Bulacan was known for bone inlay on dark wood. Because of the heat and humidity, *solihiya* (a woven rattan mesh) substituted for upholstery when Louis XV and XVI revival furniture types and the Victorian horsehair sofa were imitated and adapted.

*T*extile arts followed a similar course of development. The earliest evidence of Philippine textiles is an *ikat*-weave of earth colors recovered from a grave site on Banton Island. Estimated to be 800 years old, the cloth indicates how old the

weaving tradition is in these islands. Early Spanish chroniclers reported that except for the *datu* (ruling class) who dressed in Chinese silk, everyone else wore homespun cotton or abaca. These fabrics were left in their natural state or dyed with a limited range of colors: earth tones, blue, and red. While communities that did not fall under Spanish hegemony persisted in weaving according to their traditions, hispanized communities like the Ilocos and the Visayas, where weaving was a major industry, adapted to colonial needs and tastes producing bedspreads, blankets, pillow cases, mosquito nets, canopies for four-poster beds, tablecloths, runners, doilies, napkins, handkerchiefs, chequered cloth for skirts, striped cloth for shirts, elaborately embroidered cloth, and so forth. European forms appeared in native weaves like the Hapsburg double-headed eagle or horse and rider, favorite motifs of weavers from Santiago in the Ilocos. Ceremonial cloths used in church services were decorated with religious motifs common throughout the Christian world: crosses, angels, religious monograms, saints.

Three generations of the Bautista clan of Malolos, Bulacan, are juxtaposed in art and photographs, along with the Holy Family in precious ivory. The family treasure is an 1870s painting of the first matriarch with her grandson by the Filipino portraitist Asuncion.

*C*olonialism did not end with the Spanish but continued for another 40 years under the USA whose influence persists to the present day. The easy adaptation of foreign forms already evident during the Spanish colonial period continued when Art Deco, Bauhaus, Scandanavian and Oriental furniture inspired local design. In the 1930s and 1940s a popular design called "ambassador" copied American Art Deco furniture and in the mid-1950s and 1960s Mies van der Rohe's Barcelona chair enjoyed wide popularity. Aspiring to an international style, the 1960s witnessed the popularity of decorative styles taken straight out of European and North American lifestyle magazines.

The late 1950s and the early 1960s saw a return to Spanish colonial forms, inspired in part by a nostalgia for cultural roots. The popularity of plastic and chrome was tempered by the desire to return to natural rather than human-made, to locally available rather than imported materials: rattan, bamboo, fibers, hardwood, leather, stone. This nostalgia prevented the total demise of artisans adept at the colonial arts. A lively cottage industry of furniture makers in Betis, Pampanga; Vigan, Ilocos Sur; Bulacan and Bohol supplied the needs of homemakers and decorators. While the weaving industry, in its death throes because of inexpensive, imported material, found a new market in the demands of decorators and interior designers.

The pervasive influence of colonialism in the decorative arts cannot be denied; after all four hundred years is a very long time in which to define taste. Nonetheless, this influence is not a chain that binds modern-day Filipino designers, artisans or homemakers. If anything, the colonial experience has enriched the choices of the contemporary designer. Decoration rather than emptiness, elaboration rather than simplicity characterizes the decorative ethos of the Filipino, and we can trace a connection for these tastes to the Filipino cultural experience which has been nothing less than rich.

Behold the fanciful Door of Angels and Cherubs, the entrance to a charming turn-of-the-century garden in Intramuros. Whimsy plays its role too in the evolution of Filipino style.

Santos

Santos are both a devotional handiwork and prized collectibles from Spanish period homes. Since the 1850s, a crucifix of Christ and a statue of the Virgin Mary were necessary in all island homes. Today santos, carved saint-figures, are displayed as domestic decoration and as art. These Christian images started off as teaching aids—but have since fostered an intimacy between Filipino believers and their blessed intermediaries. The expert collectors say there's definitely a certain beauty in old santos that one cannot define. "The nostalgia they evoke . . . the feelings they conjure. They exude an unmistakable forcefulness." Especially in ivory, santos are an exquisite art. The ivory heads of santos were carved separately from the body, with the carver often not knowing what body it would fit. Courtesy: Tony Martino, Ramon Villegas and Inigo Zobel.

Altars in the Oratorio

Religiosity extends to the home. Every traditional Filipino household has a small oratorio or chapel room, born of three centuries of Spanish Catholicism. On formal altars (as in this Gothic-style altar from Casa Manila, main picture), the family venerated their favorite santos or carved saint-images. The art of carving santos eventually evolved into a means of expression for local craftsmen who produced earthy or naive images enthroned in individual wooden altars. Meanwhile, classic santos with fine ivory heads and hands (inset) were dressed in silk and velvet. Courtesy: Tony Martino and the Montilla-Tomkins collection.

26

Bamboo and Capiz

Bamboo and capiz shell are the most common materials of rural Philippine architecture. Capiz shell is a translucent flat bivalve that dwells in the muddy sandy bottoms of the brackish waters of Southern Luzon and in (their namesake) Capiz Province on Panay Island. The flat shell is harvested, cleaned, and then trimmed into tiny panes for latticed panels—called capiz windows. Adapted from the bahay kubo, the humble capiz is now well integrated into contemporary home decor. Bamboo, the pliant and versatile grass, grows wild and plentiful in the countryside. Barely 20 percent of the country's 300 species of bamboo find their way into all aspects of Filipino life—from boats and fishing to building materials and utensils. Primarily, bamboo is the poor man's timber: hewn, shaved, beaten, trimmed, or woven for myriad uses and patterns in rustic houses and furniture.

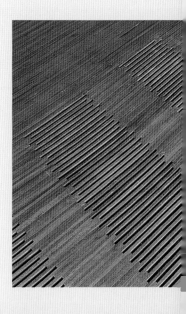

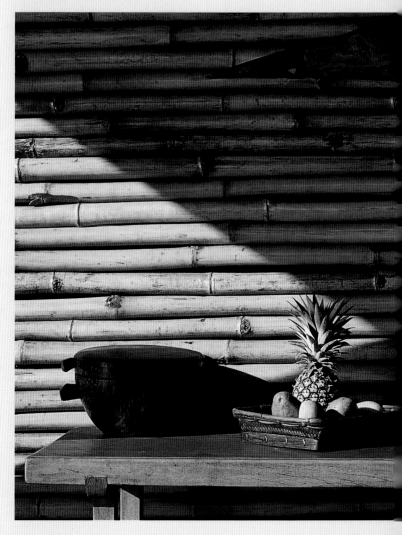

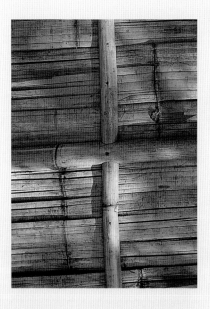

Kusina, the Kitchen

The traditional wood-fire kitchen was a hot steamy affair centered around a raised hearth of several open fires and a bulbous clay oven shaped like an igloo. (Main picture, the old-style kusina of Casa Manila in Intramuros, Manila.) Traditional culinary implements were made of wood and stone or pottery called palayok. The animal-shaped kayuran (inset) has short metal teeth used to scrape coconut meat from its shell. Bamboo and rattan baskets (right, top) were used for food storage or marketing, as well as for lunch carrying. Spiral trivets fashioned from pine needles (right, middle) coddle hot dishes. The ornate wooden blocks (right, below) are actually cookie molds imprinted with the image of San Nicholas. Biscuits baked with the saint's image were given to the sick, who nibbled cookies for health and holiness.
Courtesy: David Baradas and Richard Lopez.

30

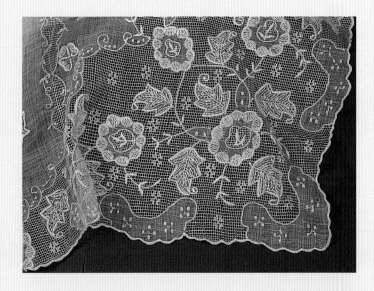

Embroidery

By Spanish times, the creative craft of embroidery was taught as part of the school curriculum and Filipino women gauged their worth by the quality of the stitching they achieved. Embroidery designs were applied to beds and tables, hand towels, baby pillows, tea towels, chemises, and children's clothes. Calado or piercing (three details, left) is the traditional style of hand-decorating that requires pulling out fibers from a certain area, strengthening the remaining ones, and then linking them together with various intricate designs. Sombrado (inset) refers to the appliqué of curvilinear patterns in white cotton over a thin cloth. Vines, leaves and flowers in very fine lines were sewn on to the fabric with practically invisible stitches, creating silhouettes of designs. Lumban, Laguna, and Taal, Batangas, are the prime Philippine embroidery centers.

Bedstead, courtesy: Manny Castro.
Embroideries, courtesy: Ramon Villegas.

Handloomed Fabrics

Lowland fabrics range from the fine and transparent to the textured and geometric. Piña is the patrician fiber, derived from a wild pineapple plant of Aklan, the piña-weaving province. Long tough pineapple fibers are gathered, washed, sorted, and woven—into piña garments that are veritable heirlooms. Sinamay is a hand-woven cloth made from the finest threads of abaca, the hemp plant. Abaca fiber is pounded to attain softness; then hand woven into transparent blouses with puffed-sleeves. Jusi, the Chinese term for raw silk, is a crisp, translucent fabric woven from local silk yarn and piña threads, the prime material of modern barong tagalogs. Silk was sometimes hand-embroidered with a fine supplementary weft. Handwoven fabrics of the north, from Ilocos to Abra, are generically called abel. Ilocanos weave a thick, textured cloth that is used mainly for blankets. Binacol is the geometric-optical design originally found in ritual blankets; while pinilian is the colorful supplementary weft weave now being revived.

Abaca and silk fabrics courtesy:
Ramon R. Zaragoza.

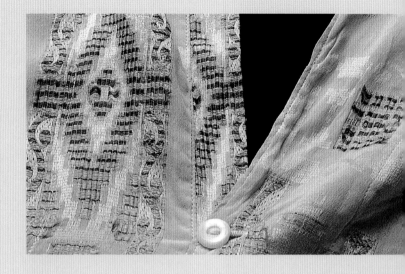

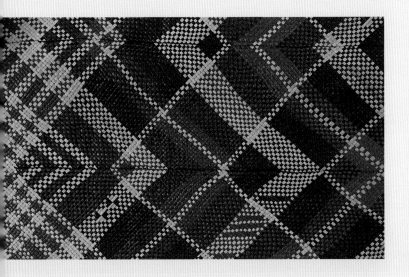

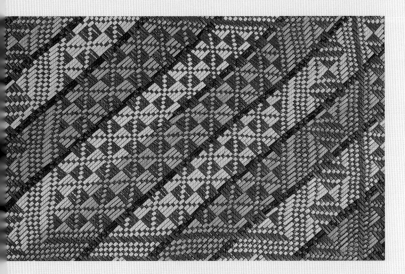

Banig, the Mat

Banig art—the folk craft of hand-weaving sleeping mats—is still very alive in Laguna, the Visayas and Mindanao. A new market for mats has opened in the export-handicraft trade. Banig are made of palm (buri), pandanus, or grass (tikog or sea grass), depending on the region. The leafy strands are dyed and selected then plaited by agile hands (helped by feet) working entirely on the floor. Designs emerge from the mat-maker's mind and go straight into the tedious process of weaving. Pictured here are geometric mats made by the shore-dwelling Samals of Sulu; with the exception of the floral mat (main picture), created by a little old lady in Magdalena, Laguna.
Courtesy: Ramon Villegas,
Ernest Santiago.

Wood

Philippine decorative arts florished throughout the eighteenth and nineteenth centuries. Filipino and Chinese artisans worked with tropical woods of many types, usually using leftovers from orders of furniture to make wooden bowls, utensils or other implements. Close-grained and dense, the woods responded well to polishing and varnishing. Craftsmen exploited the inherent beauty of these woods; their fine grains and textures were exposed in many shades. The most popular woods were: tindalo or balayong which was reddish to dark brown in color. Narra, the queen of Philippine woods, sometimes called Philippine mahogany, is fine-grained, yellowish, red or just beautiful warm brown. And kamagong displays even, alternating bands of black and brown. In the Tagalog region, Pampanga and Bulacan became the furniture-making centers; while Paete, Laguna, emerged as the woodcarving center south of Manila.

Art Nouveau Frames

Until the late 1930s, craftsmen in the Tagalog regions of Bulacan, Pampanga, Laguna and Batangas produced decorative home furnishings such as these elaborate Art Nouveau picture frames. Furniture makers would whittle frames to match a chair, bed or closet, skillfully fashioning them in various types of wood (most likely leftovers from furniture orders). These frames are unique artifacts that dazzle the onlooker with native flora such as sampaguitas, squash vines, ilang-ilang blossoms and anahaw palms; grapevines, scrolls, ink quills, and female faces with flowing hair. Patterns of mats, basketry and embroidery of saints' vestments filled the blank areas. The elegant lady framed in the main picture is a mestiza of the Gaston family. She keeps vigil in the Balay Negrense in Silay, Negros.
Courtesy: Montilla-Tomkins family, Ramon Villegas.

Silver Trays, Repoussé Frames

Distinctive silver accessories set off the tables and bureaus of yesteryear and today. On this page are: a late eighteenth century cigar holder; a mid-nineteenth century betelnut presentation tray; and an early nineteenth century fruit bowl. To the right: a silver candle-holder; and three early twentieth century silver key holders from the atelier of Crispulo Zamora in Manila. Local interpretations of fanciful key-rings incorporated the Victorian hand, musical instruments, flowers, butterflies, even the American eagle.
Courtesy: Ramon Villegas.
Main picture and inset: silver-plated brass picture frames from the atelier of Via Antica. These manufactured frames embellished with floral repoussé contain the photos one displays on pianos and occasional tables.

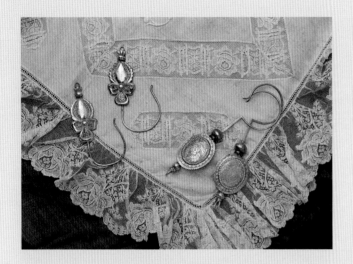

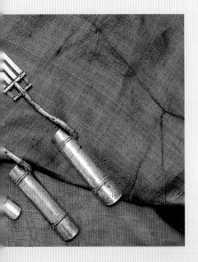

Tableware and Paliteras

Chinese immigrants brought new skills to Manila, producing fine work in gold and silver. Mostly, they copied Spanish works with exactness, especially domestic tableware of the nineteenth century, silver flatwear and holloware. Philippine-made silverware is 92 percent pure, mostly made from melted Mexican silver coins. Some silver works, clockwise from top left: nineteenth century mosquito net holders; silver key rings; a presentation set with the name of Sinforoso San Pedro, a Filipino revolutionary; and a mid-nineteenth century palitera (toothpick holder) from Apalit, Pampanga; silverware from the Arnedo family of Pampanga; and betel nut presentation trays from Pampanga, Bulacan, Laguna and Batangas.
Courtesy: Ramon Villegas.
Inset: An heirloom of Pampanga, this silver tulip palitera is provided with small holes into which the carved toothpicks may be stuck like a bouquet.

Traditional Houses

Fernando Nakpil Zialcita

"From birth, the islanders are raised in the water," wrote the Jesuit missionary Pedro Chirino in 1604 of Filipinos. "Even as children, men and women swim like fish. To cross rivers they do not need a bridge." Filipinos have organized their lives around water. Aside from immersing themselves often in the rivers and seas, they have used them as avenues between the hinterland and the coast, or between islands. Bodies of water unite Filipinos from opposite coasts rather than divide them. Moreover, much of the protein in the Filipino diet comes from aquatic life. Water too has a sacred significance. In pagan times one of the chief manifestations of divinity dwelt in the river: the crocodile who was appeased with food offerings. The names of various ethnic groups thus allude to water: Tagalog and Taosug mean the People of the River; Pampanga: The River Bank Dwellers; Ilocano: The People of the Bay; Maranao: The Lake Dwellers.

This affinity for water is reflected in the locations of many settlements, in the design of the local houses whether of farmer or townsman, and in the peculiarities of the Filipino visual style.

Traditionally, many settlements stretch along a coast or a river to make it easy for house-dwellers to wash their clothes, bathe, fish, and visit other villages via the waterways. The houses themselves are frame constructions where the floor is suspended over the ground as a precaution against floods, the humid ground, and predators. Thanks to wet rice cultivation, even the inland Filipino lives close to the water, for the fields become ponds during the planting season and are the habitat of fish, shrimps and crabs.

The house-on-stilts has a long ancestry in Southeast Asia; each area has developed its own variation. The bronze drums of Dong-son, excavated in Vietnam and Indonesia and dating from around 500 B.C., show scenes in bas-relief of village life. They include representations of houses-on-stilts.

Two variations are widely diffused throughout the Philippine islands and can be said to constitute a national style. One is the farmer's hut, called bahay kubo, which is still in use throughout the rural areas of the archipelago; the other is the towndweller's house, the wood-and-stone house, or bahay na bato at kahoy, originally built during colonial times and continually revised since then. The plans of both styles relate to the Filipino method of organizing the world.

Posts in traditional rural houses use either hardwood or bamboo. The area they define can be as small as three by two-and-a-half meters and is often enlarged by adding extensions. The tiebeams that support the roof hover around two to two-and-a-half meters above the floor. The framework for the roof is generally made of bamboo. The steeply pitched roof is propped up by four corner rafters and rows of minor rafters. Roofs are either gable or four-sided. Sometimes a kingpost strengthened with cords is used to stabilize the roof frame. Slats are laid on the rafters to carry the thatch shingles which are tied to them with rattan lashings. There is no ceiling. The house floor rises one to two meters above the ground. A wooden or bamboo frame supports joists which in turn carry bamboo floors with spaces in between the bamboo for easy cleaning. The walls are essentially sidings made of bamboo frames and slats which are covered in a variety of ways with bamboo and thatch. Many bahay kubo are thus assembled like baskets: the sidings are often bamboo strips woven into patterns, while the floors are of spaced bamboo slats.

Light and air enter the house through large windows which are opened by pushing out bamboo panels covered with thatch shingles, through the floors and, occasionally through gaps in the woven walls. Air flows through the house continuously even on a hot day, while light suffuses the interior in a unique, soothing, diffused manner. The floor slats give light, while filtering it at the same time. This pattern is repeated in urban houses' windows, as will be shown.

The bahay kubo varies from region to region. The Ilocano version has walls made entirely of thin bamboo split down the middle and lined up in two rows facing each other in concave-convex fashion. Tagalog and Pampango bahay kubo

Man-sized santos—carved saint images—representing the Last Supper in San Miguel, Bulacan. Ownership of a holy image or tableau confers prestige on a family. The pious ensemble is decorated with lights and flowers and is brought out on Good Friday together with ensembles from other leading families. In most Filipino towns the largest processions are a social register of Who's Who.

feature either shaggy nipa shingles or else split-and-flattened bamboos woven together in herringbone patterns. The most striking construction patterns are from the Visayas. From Cebu: split-and-flattened bamboo is woven into two-toned concentric diamond shapes, dark brown on light brown. From Panay: rattan is twisted into rosette window grills or rows of bamboo half-split and bent to create intersecting and festive-looking Gothic arches. Do these differences in pattern reflect regional characteristics? Some Filipinos would say yes as the Ilocano is traditionally seen as sober; the Visayan as flirtatious; the Tagalog and Pampango as in between the two.

Bahay kubo tend to become prettier the further they are from the city. Often they are surrounded by gardens filled with flowering plants, ponds, vegetables and fruit trees. A winding path of packed earth or stone slabs leads to a modest bamboo front ladder.

*P*ublic and private spaces are carefully distinguished by this seemingly simple house. Passersby and friends dropping in for a visit are entertained either at an elevated porch at the front of the house or in a shed that extends the house. Cherished guests are invited to go further into the house, into a living room with comfortable chairs and low tables. This room merges into a dining area at the rear with a kitchen to the side. The dining area and kitchen often occupy the same space, but not always. In the kitchen there is sometimes a clay stove, lately replaced by gas. By the kitchen is an outdoor porch, called a *batalan*, for washing both cooking utensils and clothes. By day the bedrooms, called *silid*, are the most private space in the house and are found at the sides or to the rear of the house. Family valuables and clothes are kept inside free-standing closets, chests, and containers made of mat. The master of the house and his wife may choose to sleep here on beds, or they may sleep with their children on simple mats spread out on the cool bamboo slats of the open living room.

The Pastor house in Batangas City, designed in 1883 is still alive and well and bursting with music. The huge antesala was used as a social salon during colonial regimes and is the setting today of owner-lawyer Tony Pastor's classical concerts. (He also leaves the windows open for the birds to hear his morning Mozart!) Pastor keeps a little office underneath his music room, tucked amid the thick stone walls. The doors, posts, and main doors are all uneven—as good luck omens.

So hospitable is the Filipino that the guest is invited to share the family's private space at night by being given a share of the room or even of the sleeping mat. The eighteenth-century French traveler Pierre de Pagès sometimes spent the night in the homes of ordinary Filipinos while on his travels. He appreciated the simplicity of their manners: "I have sometimes found, when I awoke in the morning, that I had borrowed the half of a fine young Indian's mat, who was asleep by my side, without giving offence to her or promoting scandal in the family."

Floors within the house are of varying heights. Often the living room is slightly higher than the porch; in turn the bedroom may be a few steps higher than the living room and dining room. Through these subtle changes in elevation, spaces are carefully defined. The higher the floor level the more private the space.

Toilets are found in a separate structure behind the house. Despite bathrooms, people still often bathe by the well in the open, or swim in the nearby stream.

Pigs and carabaos may be kept under the house; or in a separate enclosure, thus freeing the house's underside as a work area. Here the men fix their fishing nets and their tools; or sort out and dry their crops such as tobacco leaves and garlic. Often the men work in the fields or at the river while the women cook, sew or attend to the children.

The bahay kubo generally accommodates only the nuclear family. But it is located beside other bahay kubo where close relatives live. Grandparents, cousins and nephews living within talking distance are only too eager to watch over Juan's and Lulu's children when the latter go to town. A Filipino child's parents are many, observed Japanese anthropologist Hiromu Shimizu, in awe. The circle of kin is also ready to help in case a sister-in-law runs out of oil while cooking; or in case a nephew needs consolation because of a fever. Should a wedding take place, the entire neighborhood, consisting of relatives and friends (who often are both), pitches in to help prepare the food for the many guests who will come, invited or not. In effect the neighborhood of many a bahay kubo is a family compound, even if there is no common fence.

Many similarities link the bahay kubo with the pre-Hispanic house-on-stilts in both structure and in the use of space. However, one cannot say that the bahay kubo has remained basically the same over the course of centuries. Compared with houses of the Cordillera and Mindanao highlanders or of the Muslims in Sulu and Mindanao, it has more and larger windows; also, as in the case of Panay, these large windows are even decorated with fancy grill-work in rattan and bamboo. In contrast, in Cordillera houses, light and air pass primarily through the doors, for, often, there are no windows. While in the great houses of Lanao, Mindanao, windows are narrow slits in the wooden walls.

One reason for these differences is that the bahay kubo of lowland Luzon and the Visayas developed side by side with another type of house: the wood-and-stone house.

After the Spaniards made Manila their capital, they initially built in bamboo and thatch. But a fire swept through the new settlement in 1583. They consequently decided to build, as in their new cities in the Americas, using cut stone, bricks and tile. The stone came from ancient, dried-up lava flows in Makati, now Metro Manila's premier business district. Bricks and tiles were made from local clay, thanks to the skill of recent Chinese settlers who came from another ancient city culture. But indigenous Filipinos quickly learned how to handle cut stone; indeed the master mason of the thick walls of Manila's walled city was most likely a native-born Filipino. The large palaces of Intramuros, decorated with iron grills, won praise from visitors. However, the Philippine environment decreed a change in the Spanish-inspired

49

architecture. Strong earthquakes in the middle of the seventeenth century destroyed many stone houses. The advantages of the native style of construction were rediscovered. Because indigenous houses had multiple joints and because their roofs rested on firmly planted wooden pillars that swayed with each shock, instead of being rigid, they generally survived earthquakes intact. A wedding between two architectural styles took place with happy results.

The new Philippine urban home had a huge roof of curved tiles supported by a system of trusses that were propped up by kingposts and struts. Rather than sitting on stone walls the framework was mortised-and-tenoned to wooden pillars, called *haligi*, that were planted deep into the ground like the legs of a table. As they needed to be solid and incorruptible, the pillars came from the molave forests. The number of stories was reduced to two. Cut stone was often restricted to the ground story and was no longer used to carry loads. Wood was preferred for the upper story walls. The pillars were either embedded in the thick stone walls or else stood freely beside them. Government decrees after earthquakes in 1863 and 1880 dictated that pillars stand by, instead of inside, the walls so as not to crack the latter. The eaves of the houses rose from the ground to a grand height of seven to eight meters. Generally, houses had at least three bays each about five meters apart.

Though there were Chinese artisans resident in the Philippines from the seventeenth century onwards, rarely do roofs have curving ridges or upturned corner eaves. But Chinese influence can be detected in windows. Philippine wooden window panels using latticework in grid patterns, such as can still be seen in houses in parts of China, appeared with this difference: in China, thick rice paper was applied to the latticework, whereas in the Philippines, flat translucent capiz shells were inserted into the gaps. The shell-panes gave, and continue to give, Filipino houses a special atmosphere. The idea of making these panels slide in grooves, instead of pushing out like conventional European windows, probably came from the Japanese who settled in Manila during the early seventeenth century, either as traders or as Christian refugees from religious persecution in their homeland. There too, as in China, latticework panels were pasted with rice paper. The difference is that Japanese panels slide.

Filipino windows thus look unique vis-a-vis the rest of Southeast Asia and Spanish America. In other traditional Southeast Asian houses, shuttered door-length panels push out from or close over tall windows protected by waist-high bannisters. The panels hang from the façade like flapping wings. In Spanish America, doors open onto cantilevered balconies. Both Southeast Asian and Spanish American window openings are vertical and narrow. In contrast Filipino windows are long and horizontal and give insiders a panoramic view of the surroundings. Philippine windows provide more options for modifying the flow of light and air. Behind the shell panels is another row of panels, wooden shutters, that are adjusted according to need. Below the wooden casement is a small window, called a *ventanilla*, protected by either wooden balusters or iron lacework grills and closed from behind by wooden panels sliding in floor grooves. Because the turn-of-the century Filipino house is an open frame, the renowned Spanish painter and Manila resident Fernando Zobel de Ayala compared it to a "gigantic bird cage".

To attract more light, the exterior wall between the crossbar above the door or window and the ceiling has more capiz panels. Seen from the street, when lit up at night, the entire upper façade glows like a paper lantern. Other houses have glass panes, either tinted or frosted. These generally do not appear earlier than the late nineteenth century when glass became cheaper than ever before.

The wood-and-stone style emerged in the late seventeenth century and spread throughout the hispanized areas of the Philippine Archipelago; it was used by lay people and clerics alike for their residences. It persisted into the nineteenth and early twentieth centuries. Its long life can be attributed to its practical yet elegant solution to the challenges posed by the environment. The steeply sloping roof shed copious rainwater and, at the same time, allowed the heat within the rooms to float easily upwards. The generous roof eaves, aided by graceful metal canopies, protected the windows from the slashing rain and the blinding heat. Cantilevered by means of the wooden framework, the upper story protected the lower story from the elements, and, moreover, seemed to spread and float of its own accord. Mention has been made of the unique windows. Inside the house, panels between transom and ceiling were pierced and carved with traceried flowers and vines, again to allow more light and air. The tracery gave added grace to the interiors.

The house held fast during earthquakes because of the strong wooden pillars supporting the roof. Spanish engineer-architects brought over to the Philippines after the earthquake of 1880 recommended using the local system of construction with its wooden pillars and minimal use of stone walls precisely because it responded better to repeated shocks.

The Tutuban Railway Station (below, left) is an Industrial-Age landmark in Tondo, Manila. Tutuban is one of the few remaining examples of "semi-Victorian Neoclassical" architecture of the 1880s, with floral ornamentation and cast-iron columns with ornate pillar caps.
Below, right: Sta. Maria Church in Ilocos Sur (see also pages 18-19).

In the provinces, these pillars were often untrimmed and allowed to twist upwards. This may have been the result of indigenous and Chinese tastes converging, preferring the natural to the overly finished. Both forest and sea thus come together in Philippine interiors: the spontaneously curving tree trunk and the broad expanse of shell windows whose mood shifts with the light. Another defining characteristic of Filipino interiors is the *volada* or hanging gallery. Because the second floor projects beyond the posts, a gallery opens between the posts and the windows, partially framing the room, and increasing its sense of intimacy.

But the construction of the roof posed problems that were never fully resolved. In order to lessen the threat of fire, the roof was constructed of tile rather than thatch. Curved tiles, however, laid in three heavy layers in a concave-convex fashion on the roofwork, sometimes fell in during earthquakes. Many households therefore, even in town centers like Taal and Bustos, used thatch even if the rest of the house was made of wood-and-stone. After the strong earthquake of 1880, the government discouraged the use of curved tiles and encouraged instead two alternatives: galvanized iron or flat tiles. Because it was cheaper, the former became more popular—and continues to raise the temperature in many Philippine homes.

Wood-and-stone houses are situated in urban centers. Sometimes they stand cheek-by-jowl with other houses. At other times, they have gardens around them. Where the situation permits, they have two entrances, a street gate and a river gate. Until the 1920s, Manila was a city of waterways. Provincial traders entered the city through estuaries that led to the Pasig River, the river that divides the city in half. Traders sold their products at the quays of the houses. When deep, the waterways brought processions as well, particularly in the provinces. During the fiesta the community's saint was (and still is) carried by boat through the settlement under the shelter of ornately decorated, towerlike structures made of bamboo and wood, aptly called pagoda.

*T*he wood-and-stone house is the logical heir to the pre-hispanic house. It perpetuates many of its features while adding others. In both, living areas tend to be confined to the upper story. Considered too damp to live in, the stone-walled ground floor is used for storing furniture and the processional carriages of saints. Rooms on both sides of the entry hall serve as office or storage space. However, at least in Manila, the first story walls narrowed because of better building techniques and became less humid. Households became larger. Eventually, rooms in the ground story became dwelling spaces, conveniently lifted above the ground to protect the inhabitants against the constant humidity and the threat of an enthusiastic monsoon season.

A wooden stairway within the house ascends from the entry hall in two stages to the rooms above. The wide stairway has bannisters featuring turned balusters or, sometimes, traceried panels. Strangers and mere acquaintances are received in a hall, called the *antesala* or *caida*, decorated with chairs and tables. Intimates are brought into the *sala*, the drawing room beside the antesala on the streetside of the house, featuring sofas with cool seats woven from rattan, and marble-topped tables. The walls and ceilings are decorated with hung paintings and *trompe l'oeil* murals of gardens and garlands, for the nineteenth century saw many excellent Filipino painters eagerly wielding their brushes.

On the street-side too are the bedrooms. They have four poster beds and elaborately carved closets and chests. The most private part of the house is the master's bedroom, for here the family valuables are kept, one of them being the life-sized saint's image that is brought out for processions. This habit of keeping processional images in the bedroom is a Filipino trait that surprises Hispanics, for in their countries, such images are owned by either the local church or by the confraternities. (Interestingly enough, in pre-hispanic times the mummified corpse of the datu was invoked as a guardian spirit and kept in a coffin in the innermost

A sad grilled window on the past. The Hizon house was a remarkable Art Deco mansion of San Fernando, Pampanga—a fanciful, sugar-built and sugar-coated bahay na bato. But with Mount Pinatubo's eruption in 1991 the house was engulfed by mud-flows (called lahar) and the Hizon family were forced to abandon their heirloom.

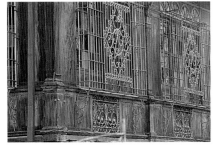

Some corners of provincial towns look just as they did in the past. But such scenes are fast disappearing under the wrecker's ball. The typical traditional townhouse used stone in the ground floor and wood with shell windows on the second floor. Because the upper level seems to fly past the second floor, the extended area, a covered balcony, is called the volada.

The Agoncillo house, a restored relic of revolutionary days in Taal, Batangas, heritage village of Southern Luzon. The 1896 bahay na bato contains a stunning dining room suite dominated by the Philippines' first-class narra and molave woods—under a stylish archway that matches the furniture.

room to protect the household.) This habit increases the prestige of the leading families; during the procession, the entire town knows who owns the most magnificent image of ivory and brocade. It also creates an opportunity for earning spiritual merit: before the procession a family is expected to display its processional image in the sala and feed all who come up to show reverence.

To the rear of the house, on the other side of the antesala, is the dining room, the *comedor*, which houses a long table with many chairs and glass cabinets that display china and cutlery. The dining room is not always separate it can be an extension of the antesala or the kitchen. Despite this, it is probably the most used area in the house. Filipinos love to eat throughout the day, especially when guests are around. Home is where the Filipino does his entertaining. Going to cafés or pubs to play cards or to chat is alien to most Filipinos. Cooking in the kitchen used to be done on a long clay stove, eventually on a gas stove. In provincial kitchens, the slatted floors of the bamboo-and-thatch house are repeated, though in sturdier form. There are no floor boards; instead one walks on wooden joists placed close together. The refuse is easily swept onto the unpaved ground below.

The kitchen opens into the batalan's heir, the *azotea*, a stone terrace with ceramic balusters which, in turn leads to the toilets and bathrooms. The azotea is an open space where washing and some of the food preparation is done. It can also be turned into a garden of potted plants which overlooks a garden or a courtyard below.

In southern Spain and Mexico, houses are built around a central courtyard. Such a fully enclosed courtyard is absent in many Filipino homes. One reason is that the many wide openings inherent in the construction of the house bring in enough light and air; another is that the L-shape of some houses creates a garden at the rear.

Traditional Filipino houses are large because families were large; often the married children stayed at home until they had a house of their own. Privacy was thus minimal. Indeed that age-old habit of laying out straw mats in any part of the house that was dry and cool prevailed even in these houses. Entire families slept cozily together on the floor by the half-opened ventanillas.

During the nineteenth century the wood-and-stone style developed two tendencies. On the one hand, it sought to enlarge its wall openings—windows and ventanillas became wider, the partition wall tracery became longer. On the other hand, it became more elaborate—floral motifs were incised or appliquéd on the exterior walls, shaped on the windows' iron grills, carved on the corbels, or cut out as roof finials. Generally, however, the decorations were discreetly applied with plenty of blank and, therefore, restful spaces around them.

At the same time, variations appeared according to region. In Ilocos, especially in Vigan which boasts the densest collection of eighteenth-nineteenth century houses, the style became brick in both stories, perhaps because of the threat of fire in the commercial district. Brick walls encased the wooden pillars all the way up to the eaves and were coated with plaster tinted with pastel shades. Sometimes the brick walls bore loads. The exteriors had little ornament: pilasters, either singly or in twos, to divide the bays; cornices consisting of a series of continuous molded lines. Despite the absence of classical capitals, the exteriors exuded a classical dignity. Inside the house, the doors had clusters of reedlike lines in ovals or diamonds carved on them. The no-nonsense air of this variation fits in with the popular image of the Ilocano.

Filipinos call their wood-and-stone houses either "Spanish" or "Antillan" because of the mistaken notion that they originated either in Spain or the Antilles in the Caribbean. Ironically, Spanish, Cuban and Mexican architects ask in puzzlement: "What is so Spanish about them?" To use a parallel example: should the Filipino *barong tagalog* be called "Spanish" just because it resembles the Central American *guayabera* (in being a collared and cuffed longsleeved shirt that is worn over the pants)? Obviously not. For, the barong tagalog, like the wood-and-stone house, differs in its being translucent in its materials (piña or jusi fiber) and traceried in its embroidery.

*A*t the turn of the century, new technologies entered the islands: reinforced concrete and American clap-boarding. The former encouraged homeowners to build all-concrete buildings that could easily withstand both quakes and fires, the latter resulted in all-wood houses. The twentieth century has seen the appearance of a wide variety of alternatives to the wood-and-stone style. One such alternative, according to the art historian Rodrigo D. Perez, is the *tsalet* (from the word "chalet"). Appearing around the 1900s, this house comprises a single story raised slightly above the ground, constructed in reinforced concrete and wood. A distinguishing feature is the extended verandah in front approached by either an L-shaped or a T-shaped stair. Bedrooms are laid out on a row on one side perpendicular to the front; living and dining rooms and the kitchen are laid out on the other. The tsalet was an attempt to create a less formal dwelling design. Even more informal are the increasingly popular "California" style bungalows and split-level houses currently being built. As this century has flowed on, the wood-and-stone style has ceased to be the preferred ideal for the urban centers. It stopped being used as a style after World War II.

The defining qualities of Filipino style are not easy to spot if one approaches our architecture with the notion that: "Since the Philippines is an Asian country, it must look non-Western. It should look exotic." Such an approach is unfair and will inevitably prevent one from discovering and enjoying the attractions of Filipino style. Any discussion of a "national style" is fraught with risk and complications, for styles vary according to locality, ethnicity, social class and historical period. Nonetheless there are two stylistic themes that do recur in all the houses I have described.

The art critic Emmanual Torres sees "cornucopia baroque" as a defining characteristic of the Filipino visual style, whether in folk art, paintings or buildings. This tendency crowds an extravagant variety of shapes and colors into a compact space, resulting in a feeling of abundance and surfeit. Indeed, nineteenth-century houses are veritable gardens in wood and stone. Let us note, however, that this exuberance is always kept within bounds by an implicit grid. Decorations, whether appliquéd or incised, are separated from others by unornamented zones which allow the eye to rest. Filipino art tends to emphasize shape through linework rather than volume. This might be due to the experience of working with basket-like house interiors, or to the fact that Filipino church and house interiors rely a great deal on painting, rather than on bas reliefs and sculptures, to create a sense of richness. The supposed Filipino "baroque" has a light, lyrical feel.

During the 1850s Filipino houses were simply decorated. Sir John Bowring, a traveler and writer, was pleased that the rooms were "not, as often in England, overcrowded with superfluities." However, with increasing prosperity the Victorian mania for overcrowding did appear. Still, the better preserved house interiors in the provinces today do exhibit the qualities that Bowring praised.

The Nakpil-Bautista house is one of the well preserved refined homes in Quiapo, old Manila. Designed in 1914 by Arcadio Arellano for Dr. A. Bautista, the house motifs were inspired by a Viennese Secession furniture set given to Dr. Bautista. All the pierced panels and window grills were custom designed.

Another aspect of Filipino style has yet to be recognized. This is what I call "a fondness for the translucent". Filipino creations love to half-reveal and half-conceal forms and colors. Capiz windows pretend to block off the outside world but actually reveal aspects of it. Capiz catches the shadow of a branch swaying outside. The moods the shell panels create change as the sun passes: at one moment, they are quiet and still; at another they shimmer like the sea at noon. The oily smoothness of the wooden floors, often uncarpeted, reflect changes in the light and give the visitor a sensation of walking on water. Similarly the cloth favored for the upper garments of the national dress for men and women is made of translucent, rather than opaque, materials: sinamay is made from loosely woven abaca, jusi is made from Chinese silk and pineapple, piña from pineapple gauze. The barong tagalog delicately reveals the torso, while at the same time concealing it. Here, as in the wood-and-stone house, the Filipino fondness for open tracery, called calado, adds elegance while daring the eye to explore the field.

What encourages this fondness for the translucent? Perhaps the ways in which Filipinos conceptualize their relations with others gives us a clue. Filipinos feel the need to be with other people and can tolerate crowding, among family members or among friends, because this creates a sense of intimacy. Wanting nonetheless to protect their own space and respect that of others, Filipinos take an indirect route: words are carefully chosen, even when expressing strong feelings, so as not to hurt other people. Sometimes teasing words may in fact be an expression of hurt feelings. Among Filipinos, words and gestures also reveal and conceal. Another clue may lie in the heat and humidity of the Philippines. Filipinos respond to this climate by making their clothes and their homes more open. Finally, the landscape of the Philippines cannot be ignored: the streams, rivers, bays, rice paddies and fishponds on which so many people's needs depend. These clear bodies of water reflect the sky, while revealing a whole world beneath the surface. Traditional Philippine houses, especially the wood-and-stone style, have responded to the Filipinos' universe and, at the same time, have framed it.

The bahay na bato in her fanciest dress—in the Visayas, of course, a region famous for her graciousness. Though ornately decorated, the façade's design is not vulgar. The Spanish called houses like this Carcar confection, the "Arquitectura mestiza", a mixed hybrid. Carcar is a town south of Cebu City with joyously decorated houses.

Following pages: Dona Gema Crisologo Street in the heritage village of Vigan, Ilocos Sur. The massive presence exuded by Vigan houses sets them apart from the rest of the country. They had an evolution all of their own: brick walls 24 inches thick rise from the street right up to the roof. Façades had pilasters for added dignity, but no decoration, no excess. Vigan streets bear the regional character of the Ilocano: sober and dignified, restrained and austere.

Elite Colonial Traditions

From the 1850s onwards, the sugar trade brought affluence to Central Luzon. Landlords' townhouses became grand and elaborate affairs— as this elegant dowager of an Ilusorio mansion on the road through Bulacan (main picture). The local gentry adapted ideas and materials from Europe and expressed their taste in their haciendas. They incorporated a grand front porch, classical Doric motifs, and French windows or imported etched-glass panes (below), in place of ordinary capiz. The brass knocker shaped like a hand (below left) was a status symbol in old towns.

Awnings and Archways

This showy abode (or Victorian Cake House) in San Miguel, Bulacan, (right) has metal cutwork awnings and fancy grills within its ventanillas—but why three stories? The story goes like this: a macho farmer married the landowner's daughter. To out-do his father-in-law, the farmer built the tallest house in the area: so that the father, on passing the threshhold, had to look up to his son-in-law! The third level housed a massive ballroom where the elite would throw balls as entertainment between sugar crops. Left: The wooden grid lines used in this porch archway are an interesting interpretation of a Chinese motif, seen in Laoag, Ilocos Norte. Below left: The window grill that's rounded like a belly—so one could put flowers or pillows within—are called rejas na buntis (pregnant grills).

Windows on the Past

Filipinos created their own windows on the world. The Art Deco balcony with receded windows (left) belonged to artist-philanthopist Dr. Luis Santos of Bulacan. His house traces the 1930s transition from Art Nouveau (nymphs in the garden) to fanciful Art Deco. Interiors feature Amorsolo paintings on ceilings, sun-patterns on the floor; reliefs and paintings of nymphs on the transoms. A Bulacan implosion of decorations! Right: A decorative approach belongs to the Lizares colonial mansion in Negros—continuous moldings, capiz windows and stylized pillars below; with balustered ventanillas and glass panes above. Right, below: Here's a more sober view of the all-wood and capiz window typical of Central Luzon.

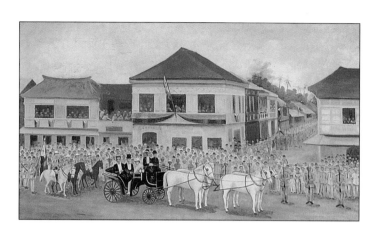

Aguinaldo's Last Shrine

The Aguinaldo Shrine in Kawit, Cavite, is the eclectic, architectural and historical legacy of General Emilio Aguinaldo (left, top right), militant leader of the 1896 Revolution and first President of the Philippine Republic (1898). The house is the creation of a patriot and a self-made architect: Aguinaldo expanded his residence into a "striking engineering wonder of eclecticism", borrowing forms and period designs and orchestrating them himself during his 50 surviving years after the revolution. Additions and extensions were styled along American Colonial lines. From the redesign of the historic Declaration Window in 1919 (left, main picture); to the addition of a five-storied, gabled and spired tower (right); to the annexing of another two-story wing. All elements of the house project patriotism, authority, power and victory—qualities which express General Aguinaldo's personality.

A Patriot's Creation

The Kawit house showcases the finest artistry and craftsmanship of the period in its gleaming wood floors, the paneled narra partitions, and the highly decorative and motif-filled ceilings. There are symbolic ornamentations in the furniture. There is a grand dining table to entertain 18 guests (who always wondered if Aguinaldo's ceiling-relief of the Philippine Islands may land in their soup). There are special function rooms, secret passages, hideaways and gadgetry. On the ground floor a small opening leads to a basement air raid shelter. There's also a bowling alley of fine hardwood downstairs. Aguinaldo gifted his house to the country in 1963. Today it is one of the best maintained landmarks and historical museums in the country.

The Taal Tradition

The town of Taal, Batangas, burgeoned during the Spanish colonial era with a history boasting revolutionary fervor and a grand lifestyle among its Batangueno aristocrats. In the 1970s, Taal refurbished her old façades in a fit of nationalism, especially around the town plaza. The two Montenegro houses (right) show off the picturesque wrap-around capiz windows and square symmetry of the Geometric Style, with the typical medallions-on-the-transom fitted with diagonally latticed capiz. Left: The huge Basilica of San Martin on Taal's plaza is the largest church in all Asia, with its boxy, two-story façade standing since 1865–although mortared only with lime and ground oyster shells! On the symmetrical plaza stands a statue of Dona Marcela Agoncillo, who made the first Filipino flag in the revolutionary days of 1896.

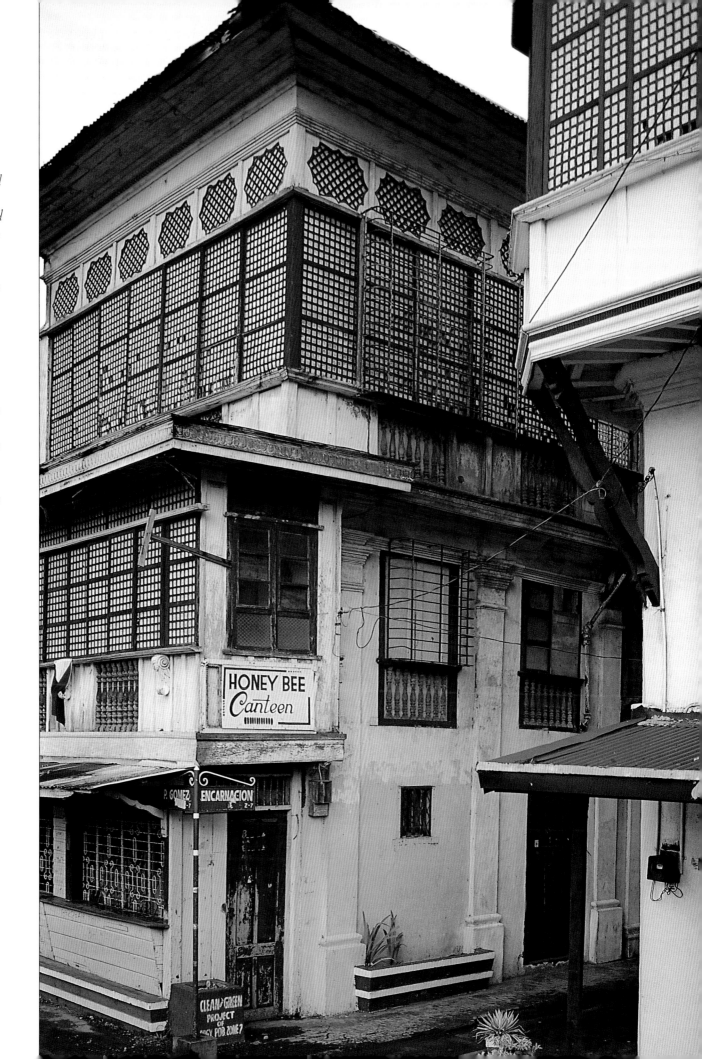

Grande Dame of Vigan

The sole intact mansion in Vigan is the 1830s
vintage house of Don Enrique Quema; in the
1920s this Chinese trader vowed to preserve the
house for posterity. The Spanish-Filipino house is
a solid structure of narra, yakal, and molave within
brick walls. Inside is a fine array of imported
Vienna bentwood furniture among Ilocos cane and
capiz items. The grand staircase balustrade is
reeded and turned–reminiscent of Georgian
England. A most curious feature of the house is
the secret peeping hole on the second level, through
which the owners screened people before
they were invited in.

Bulacan's Caryatid House

In the late 1900s the homes of the gentry were status symbols importing ideas and themes from everywhere. Sugar landowners erected the tallest roofs and the most elaborate decoration; carving was used extensively and Victorian overcrowding characterized interiors. The Bautista Caryatid House was built in the 1850s and redecorated in 1877: a frothy confection of French Art Nouveau with nouveau baroque details. As the Bautista patriarch was an aide to hero of the revolution General Emilio Aguinaldo, the family entertained in style. The modern-day ceiling is painted with nymphs and nyads; while memorabilia is juxtaposed with religious art. The exterior is unique: there are four white caryatids perched on the white façade; and frosted French glass windows, not capiz, between the baroque columns. Patriarch-artiste Dez Bautista offers: "Maybe Bulakenos are just more flamboyant in their homes, than in their speech and cuisine—as are the Pampanguenos!"

Agoncillo House, Taal

Taal, Batangas, situated on a hillock overlooking
Balayan Bay, is striving to be recognized as a
Tagalog heritage village in Southern Luzon. Near
the bottom of Taal's slope, is an all-white bahay
na bato built in the 1890s. Here lived Felipe
Agoncillo, revolutionary hero and diplomat, and
Dona Marcela Agoncillo, the maker of the first
Filipino flag. The restored living room
(main picture) still arrays a wide range of capiz
shell, forming a continuous corner-to-corner
screen. The glistening squares cast their muted
glow upon "Ambassador" armchairs of
the 1940s.

Apacible House, Taal

The Apacible house is as interesting as
its historical memorabilia. Superficially
Americanized and dressed in
Commonwealth finery, her Filipino
identity still prevails. Four generations
ago, Maria Diokno built her house on a
beautiful site near Taal Church. Her
granddaughter Matilde married the
revolutionary ilustrado Leon Apacible–
whose name stayed with the house.
After being widowed, Matilde married
Vicente Noble, Governor of Batangas.
In 1938, the house was remodelled by
an architect from Lemery, Batangas,
who introduced an Art Deco motif of
three interlocking triangles–signifying
V. This motif appears everywhere: in
the floor parquetry, in the vents above
doors, on all window grills, even carved
into furniture. Its repetition visually ties
the whole house together with an
updated American Art Deco feel.
The Apacible Museum today contains
the family memorabilia of
three generations.

Casa Gorordo, Cebu

This colonial bahay-na-bato of 1863 belonged to the first Filipino Bishop of Cebu, Juan Gorordo. One century later, the Ramon Aboitiz Foundation of Cebu bought the bahay to showcase an ilustrado home at the turn of the century. In 1085 the Gorordo mansion was fully restored and opened as a museum by Architect Augusto Villalon. The bahay comprises a stone-walled ground floor and family living quarters above; a tile roof with Chinese upturned eaves; wooden sidings and capiz windows upstairs. The house also has an unusual trellised second-floor patio running the length of the house beside the living area. Inside the Cebuano character is reflected in the design: frivolous, flirtatious, festive-looking with Gothic arches; and some would say, gently feminine.

Painted House of Carcar

The hand-decorated Silva house in the hill-town of
Carcar outside Cebu was designed by Benito Silva
and Rev. Fr. Anastasio del Corro in 1883. The
two friends gathered materials from one old house
in Naga, Cebu; and from the old del Corro house
in Carcar. The artisans are remembered by their
work—the carpenter who carved the doors was
called Basilio from Sibonga, Cebu, the painter
of the fine details was Pongardas from Carcar.
In 1898 the Rev. Fr. Filomeno Silva celebrated
his first Mass in this house.

Bahay na Tisa, Carcar

This 1850 ancestral house was the first stone structure in Carcar, Cebu—built alongside Carcar Church. In 1980, when it was designated for demolition, the old house was saved by two fifth-generation descendants. Bit by bit over four years interior designer Manny Castro invested in rebuilding and refurnishing his grandmother's house: re-laying floors, reinforcing the roof, painting, accessorizing, decorating. As the house is unique for its use of the original brick tile roofing—tisa—Castro named his house-reborn, Bahay na Tisa (House of Tiles). The centerpiece and reason for Castro's annual return to Carcar is a life-size image, Santo Sepulcro, acquired from Spain when the house was built. The image is celebrated every Good Friday, when Castro returns home and fêtes friends with the revived richness of Carcar's bygone age.

"Balay Negrense", Silay

When Silay was the economic and cultural center of Negros, sugar scion Victor Gaston constructed one of the biggest colonial homes on the island. From 1901-1927 he lived there with his 12 children in six bedrooms on each floor; with their basketball court-sized living room upstairs; a grand W-shaped stairway; calado or carved panels that were ventilators between rooms; etched window glass, fancy-grilled ventanillas and sprawling gardens.

The Gaston house was reborn as
the Balay Negrense house-museum
in 1987, under the Negros Cultural
Foundation. Floors were restored,
furniture reset, walls painted in the
tones of yesteryear. The Balay Negrense
was followed similarly by the
Bernardino-Jalandoni house-museum nearby.
This house was built in 1912 and displays
embossed steel trayed ceilings imported from
Hamburg, Germany; and fine collections of books,
glassware and lace supplied by Silay Heritage
Foundation members.

Hacienda Heritage

The Montilla-Tomkins hacienda house is an outstanding example of the provincial bahay na bato built with local materials. The lower floor is made of coquina, a coral rock that's difficult to harvest. The upper story is cantilevered by means of woodwork inside, so it seems to spread and float of its own accord and leaves an overhanging balcony area, called the volada. Within the coral walls are six massive wooden pillars stretching from ground to roof; trunks whole and untrimmed—the spontaneous angling responds better to the shocks of earthquakes. Generous roof eaves, aided by metal canopies, protect the windows from slashing rain and blinding heat. Left: the grand sala or living room is much as it was designed in 1852 by haciendero Don Agustin Montilla from Cordoba, Spain.

Montilla-Tomkins Hacienda

Set proudly apart amidst the cane fields of Ubay, Negros,
the sugar hacienda today contains the heirlooms and
personal collections of the present owner, Herbert
Montilla-Tomkins. Antique furniture crowds the mansion
bedrooms with the memories of five generations. The four-
poster bed is said to be an original work of the Chinese
furniture maker Ah Tay. Portraits of the Montilla heirs
straddle a regal mirror of Manila-worked etched glass
(right). The Philippine Empire cane-weave divan
beneath was a settee popular in the sugar-producing
regions during the mid-1800s.

Foreign Influences

Rene Javellana

T he Philippines can be compared to an artery, which many peoples traversed on their way to other destinations. This constant traffic created an environment where exchanges in style and esthetics allowed the emergence of synthetic types of art and architecture.

Although Indian culture, a pervasive influence throughout Southeast Asia, enriched the Philippine languages and left its mark in weaving crafts and oral literature, it hardly influenced architecture. But the far more distant culture of Islam did influence building, most especially in the southern Philippines. By the second half of the thirteenth century, a few principalities of Southeast Asia had converted to Islam and Muslim traders coming to the Philippines from as far away as Oman established settlements among the indigenous peoples of the Sulu Archipelago and Mindanao. In time missionaries arrived to reinforce the faith that the traders had brought. The tomb of Tahun Maqbalu who died in 710 A.D. or 1310 A.D. is cited as evidence of Muslim presence, and possibly of a vibrant and permanent Islamic settlement.

Islamic influence manifests itself in the dominance of abstract and colorful surface decorations found in the Maranao *torogan* or clan house, the *masjid* or mosque and the *ranggar* or *langgal* or prayer hall. Called *okir* by the Maranao and *ukkil* by the Tausog of Sulu these decorations are abstract natural forms like the *naga* or snake or the *pako rabong* or fern.

Although Sung annals report traders from Ma-i (possibly Mindoro in the Philippines) arriving in Canton in 982 A.D. and although Chinese tradeware from the Tang Dynasty has been recovered from ancient burial sites—evidence of a flourishing trade with China prior to European colonization—Chinese influences on Philippine architecture and living spaces did not appear until the colonial period when the Spanish employed Chinese artisans and master builders in construction. Establishing colonies in Cebu in 1565, Panay in 1569 and Manila in 1571, the conquistador Miguel Lopez de Legazpi laid the foundations of the colonial network. Because none of the Spanish colonizers were architects colonial architecture barely differed from indigenous bamboo and thatch dwellings for two decades. But, after a fire razed Manila in 1583, the colonists sought ways to build more permanent structures using stone and mortar. Credit for introducing European architectural traditions and techniques is customarily given to the friars and missionaries who combined religious duties with the more mundane task of building. Native and Chinese artisans worked for the colonists. By 1595, the bishop of Manila, Domingo Salazar, reported that Chinese merchants had a flourishing trade selling bricks, tiles and other construction material so that it was no longer necessary to import materials from Mexico, this being too expensive.

While early stone and mortar habitations were patterned after Western and Mexican models, a series of disastrous earthquakes in the seventeenth century fostered a distinctive house type while the participation of native and Chinese artisans in construction set the stage for a synthesis. Chinese influence is notable in the curved silhouette of the tile roof, the wooden hinges and locks, the translucent window panes made from capiz and the use of Chinese elements for decorations and furnishing—fu dogs, lions, scroll-like clouds, dragon-like scroll work, geometric lattice screens—the list is endless.

Colonialism was not merely an exercise in political and economic domination but also an experiment in cultural exchange. By establishing the galleon trade between Mexico and the Philippines, Spain created an umbilical cord through which Western styles and tastes could come to the Philippines while Eastern artistic traditions came to be known, copied and emulated in Europe. Adapted to and modified by Philippine realities and sensibilities, the European artistic movements found an echo in the Spanish colony. One can rightly speak of periods of colonial art, namely: Baroque (seventeenth and eighteenth century); Rococo (c. 1780); Revivalists (Neoclassical, neo-Romanesque; neo-Gothic; neo-Renaissance; nineteenth century).

Gothic rose windows were unique to Negros. This traceried window (1880s), built into the Lizares colonial mansion in Talisay, allowed the orchestra by the stairs to be heard in the living room. This classic nineteenth century Visayan townhouse has been preserved by its heirs with all its European airs intact.

In 1896, a revolution against Spanish rule erupted. Inspired by ideas of the European Enlightenment brought home by European-educated scions of the elite and supported by massive discontent with despotic rule, the revolution raged for two years until Spain ceded the Philippines to the United States in the Treaty of Paris of 1898. The half-century American experiment with colonialism began.

The initial American reaction to Spanish colonial architecture was to criticize it as medieval. Thus, seeking to improve infrastructure and the architecture of public buildings, Governor William Cameron Forbes, invited Daniel H. Burnham to come to the Philippines and propose urban plans for Manila and Baguio. Burnham, who had established a reputation as a city planner and architect having worked on the Chicago World's Fair of 1893 and the cities of Washington D.C., Cleveland, San Francisco and Chicago, spent six weeks visiting Manila and Baguio in 1904 . On his return to the United States he sought an architect to implement his plans. Impressed by the credentials of William E. Parsons, he recommended him as the Philippine government's consulting architect. Arriving in Manila in 1905, Parsons organized a staff of Filipino and American architects for the Bureau of Public Works. Burnham's own dictum that architects would do well to study Spanish colonial architecture for their Philippine projects was followed by the Bureau for its design of the Philippine General Hospital and of public school buildings that were built throughout the archipelago. High ceilings, wide windows, transoms and the generous use of translucent shell panes show the inspiration of colonial architecture. However, toward the end of his assignment Parsons turned to the Neoclassical style for public buildings, a style also favored by Burham, thereby crystallizing a distinct style for government buildings.

The main Post office building in Manila (above) by American-era architect Juan Arellano. The newly refurbished Champagne Room in the Manila Hotel (right).

Following pages: Manila's stately Mira-Nila mansion.

By the late nineteenth century Filipinos were already training as architects in Europe and with the establishment of the Bureau, Filipinos were sent to American architectural schools as government scholars. Exposed to other trends, these architects drew from a wider repertoire of styles including Art Nouveau and Art Deco. Art Nouveau and Art Deco found expression in theaters, offices and commercial buildings and residences. Built in 1931 and designed by Juan Arellano, the Metropolitan Theater in Manila, an amalgam of Nouveau and Art Deco styles though given a local touch with its use of tropical plants and fruits as motifs, shows the easy assimilation of this new style by Filipino architects. The American period also saw the growth of row houses and apartments, functional rather than stylish, for the growing urban population.

The Pacific War left the Philippines in a shambles. The 1950s was a period of intense rebuilding. Damaged buildings were restored though, unfortunately, much historic architecture was left to rot, like Intramuros, the ancient Spanish-built walled city of Manila. By the 1960s functional buildings in the Modernist International style became the trend, usually constructed in vast new developments. By the 1970s a search for a distinctive Philippine style, especially in residential buildings, inspired a reassessment of the indigenous and Spanish and American colonial traditions, producing modern buildings with a distinctive Filipino approach. In the 1980s and 1990s new buildings found inspiration in the eclecticism of the Postmodern movement.

Mira-Nila, Manila's Viewdeck

In 1929, the Conrado Benitez family built a
home in San Juan, overlooking Manila, naming
the manor "Mira-Nila" (also previous pages). The
Filipino-Spanish house was designed by Dona
Francesca Tirona Benitez with her maestro
(master carpenter), her foreign magazines—and
the "like this!" method. The mansion has
Revivalist traits on the front patio and Art Deco
colored glass windows in the sala. The library
(right) is a crossroads of Chinoiserie alongside
Benitez family memorabilia.

San Agustin Church

The first church in Luzon saw its beginnings in bamboo, nipa and wood, and endings in fire and earthquakes, before emerging in 1865 as the first earthquake-proof building on Philippine soil. The San Agustin Church façade is both Renaissance and Mexican in inspiration, with barrel-vaulted buildings comprising the monastery alongside the church and two Chinese Fu lions guarding the cobblestoned parking lot! Inside, chapels and buttressed walls line the nave; while ceilings glow with Italian trompe l'oeil murals. The massive stone halls and rooms of the old monastery are a repository of fine religious art as well as the majestic ecclesiastical furniture that inspired the Filipino secular furniture tradition. San Agustin's famous Baroque door is the heavily carved gateway that appears on page 16.

The Manila Hotel

The Manila Hotel, built by American William E. Parsons in 1912, is the most historic hotel in the country—the scene of the lavish events of Filipino society and the Commonwealth government, until it was almost fully destroyed during World War II. In 1975 Architect Leandro Locsin restored and extended the hotel, respecting the architecture of the hotel's historical past, while expressing the values of modern Filipinos. With interior designers Patricia and Dale Keller, Locsin gutted the dark lobby and expanded it into a three-story atrium with gleaming marble and massive columns (main picture). The Kellers found references in old architectural journals in the United States; and unearthed one Doric column buried by time. Bringing this exciting new perspective to bear, they reawakened the romance of the Commonwealth and revived the grandeur of the American-era Filipino-Spanish Manila Hotel. This page, from the top: the MacArthur Suite; the hotel exterior; and the Champagne Room (recently renovated by Conrad Onglao and Ivy Almario).

Tomas Mapua's Masterpiece

In 1911 Tomas Mapua graduated from Cornell University, New York, received Architectural License No. 1 in the Philippines, and designed the remarkable "living sculpture" that was his mansion on Taft Avenue, Manila. Until today (despite the blight of the city railway), the Mapua-Lim house is an Art Deco masterpiece in design and craftsman-ship. Decorative work includes wood and plaster relief, metal grillwork, stylized carving and inlay, hand-painting, and faux-surfacing done (in 1934) by artistic Filipino craftsmen. From the three-toned marquetry through to the sala walls covered with stylized canvases of banana and anahaw palms in sienna and green; to the ceiling that combines capiz shell lighting (by colored bulbs) and an Oriental mural depicting stylized clouds—any moment, you'd expect Lady Sarah Bernhardt to come gliding through the setting. The sala furniture is all period, with matching Chinese clouds on the upholstery.

The Romance of the Met

The Metropolitan Theater in Manila was built in 1931 by the city's gifted architect, Juan Arellano. It is his most romantic work, heavily influenced by the Art Deco movement. The monumental building barely survived World War II bombings and was partially restored in the mid-1970s; but without government support and motivation it seems doomed for demolition in the twenty-first century. Left, top: The theater façade, crowned by a curved wall ending in pinnacles, is like a proscenium itself. The entrance comprises grillwork of stylized birds-of paradise and a large window-mural of colored glass. Right: Walls are pastel and embroidered, festive and colorful. Inside are a two-story lobby, wide stairways, and Amorsolo murals; seats for 1,670 people, and four plaques depicting the saddened muses of Music, Tragedy, Comedy and Poetry.

The American Colonial Style

In the US Embassy building on the edge of Manila Bay—built circa 1935—the Neoclassical columns that were then popular in Manila have been simplified into a plain vertical colonnade (left) around the circular ballroom and reception hall (above).

The Art Deco Touch

La Salle University in Manila (right), constructed from the 1920s onwards, features stately columns and multiple balconies for the public eye. Art Deco design—by architect Tomas Mapua—found its way into the private, holy spaces (above).

A Theater for Pundaquit

Behold an alternative theater for the alternative arts: Casa San Miguel in Pundaquit, Zambales Province. Here's one man's cultural center, erected on his ancestral land in 1993. In Pundaquit by the sea, Alfonso 'Coke' Bolipata plays his classical violin and shares his culture with fellow artists in residence—and his grass-roots community. Besides his motivations as a musical returnee, 'Coke' Bolipata has imported American architectural ideas gathered in his 15 years' living in the USA.

Casa San Miguel from the outside is pure New England Shaker redone in red Ilocos brick. The performance theater (above) looks out to the greenery and upward to a great organic ceiling of bamboo. At right, grilled balconies look out on the mango orchard where 173 fruit trees have borne fruit since grandpa's days. Bolipata, who grew up as a musical prodigy in New York, credits his grandfather, Don Ramon Corpus, as the inspiration for his music as well as the Cultural Center in the Pundaquit orchard.

Filipino-Shaker in Zambales

Inside, the Casa San Miguel is playfully Filipino to the core. All in casuarina wood, the large rooms are unpainted and unexpected spaces, with Philippine-style fenestration on the sides: sliding capiz shell windows, grilled ventanillas and colored glass panes let the light and air into the residential quarters. The furniture is a mixture of grandpa's old and Bolipata's new: folk-style antique furniture sits next to avant garde woodworks (right) mostly by modernist sculptor Gerosalino Araos. Then, look up: there are stairways and balconies everywhere—demonstrating the musician-designer's love for narrow passages to hidden attic-rooms and garrets for resident artists. Pundaquit's Casa is thoroughly Filipino, with inventive intimations of Escher!

Phoenix of Pampanga

The Lazatin mansion in San Fernando, Pampanga, built in 1929, has been twice reborn like a phoenix—first from the devastation of war in 1945; then from the devastation of Mount Pinatubo's eruption in 1991. Inside, the big white colonial house is intact, integrated and elegant with a 1940s ambience. Dona Carmen Lazatin, one of three sisters living in the mansion, recounts how they rescued the house from the wrath and lahar (mudflow) of Mount Pinatubo. The whole garden was buried under five feet of ash before the lahar ceased its flow—at the edge of their street. Several large trees were sacrificed, but the Lazatins' garden has recently returned to full bloom. The view may be enjoyed, graciously, from the front verandah, dressed in decorative tiles.

Filipino-Hispanic Baroque

The sumptuous home of Eduardo and Dely Ongsiako accommodates many foreign objects: from Russian chandeliers to Hispanic religious statuary—all arrayed alongside paintings by National Artist Fernando Manansala. Mrs Ongsiako sought the help of eclectic decorator Teyet Pascual to rearrange her crowded collection of antiques and folk art. Starting with the space, Pascual pushed the living room to the garden wall; reduced the dining area to a glassed-in room; and then orchestrated antiques with souvenirs; relics with modern paintings; porcelains with figurines. The sala with a grand piano opens on to a dining terrace under a cascade of Philippine vigil lamps. The back wall garden designed by the matron's nephew, Juan Miguel Ongsiako, is landscaped on the vertical: to include lush vegetation, molave trunks, giant rocks and a water-sprinkling system that rains down with a cool shimmering effect.

The Nelly Garden House

There's a floral romance behind this elaborate mansion in the Southern Philippines. In 1928 Don Vicente Villanueva Lopez, Sr., and his wife Elena Javelona Hofileña built their European-style mansion to cater to a lifestyle that called for fabulous parties. Balls and receptions were held here, with society, Filipino and foreign, in attendance. Their eldest daughter Nelly's great love for flowers found expression in the

vast garden, then maintained by eight
gardeners; until Nelly's garden attached
its name to the whole property.
Engineer Mariano Salas built this
grand Gothic- and Deco-inspired
mansion in Iloilo on five hectares
(bought for one peso per square meter).
Burnished tindalo or rosewood was used
throughout most of the mansion—
especially in the fabulous staircase.

Filigreed House, Cebu

*By the 1930s, Art Deco had arrived on
Philippine shores in a big way. Self-motivated
homeowners did their own thing with their
maestros and local labor. They adapted materials
and ideas from everywhere, especially multi-colored
glass, stylized grillwork, trellises and gothic tracery
patterns. In 1932 a Cebuano couple, Gil Garcia
and Teresa Escano, designed their own filigreed
house. They sourced hardwoods from Dinagat
Island, off Surigao del Norte in Mindanao; and
hired all the craftsmen in town to help assemble
their dreamhouse. Colored glass panels in every
corner admitted rainbows of green, violet and gold.*

The Embroidered House

*The calado, carved, pierced wood panels
generally placed along transoms to allow air to
circulate between rooms, was developed
to its ultimate degree in this house. Calado
panels became pierced screens, filigreed dividers,
and entire wood-traceried walls. The Jose Garcia
house's landing at the top of the stairs (right)
feels like dazzling lacework in wood. Note the
one-passenger elevator fashioned to transport
elders up the steep staircase—created
in a matching Art Deco design.*

Jaro's Deco Mansion

The Sanson-Montinola mansion in Jaro, Iloilo, was custom-built for the needs of an elite family. Their lifestyle shows first in the grand sala that extends over the carriage port to have a three-way view of the neighborhood; and then in the elaborate staircase—made for the many Montinola debutantes. The large back room, once the dining room, is a symphony of Art Deco windows and the multi-hued tiles of the 1930s. The narrow spiral stairway in the corner ascends to the very private bachelor's room. Another stairway—secreted away in a bedroom closet—climbs to a pint-sized attic just under the roof, where the children were sent to play when the grown-ups had a party below.

Traditions Adapted

Augusto F. Villalon

*T*he Filipino home reflects the lifestyle that large, stone and wood houses have sheltered since the Spanish colonial era. But with the onset of modernization, the leisurely lifestyle enjoyed by earlier generations is now only a memory. During the 1970s many modern homeowners continued with tradition by evoking the ambience of the old in their contemporary settings. A nostalgic wave in architecture was established, perpetuating memories of the past and bearing traces of the ancestral lifestyle into the present. A small, enlightened slice of the private sector looked inward towards the traditions of their ancestors.

By the late 1970s several private foundations started to collect antique furniture with the aim of mounting permanent exhibitions in house-museums open to the public. In 1976, the Museo ng Buhay Pilipino, sponsored by the D.M. Guevara Foundation, was the first house-museum to showcase the furnishings and lifestyle of lowland, Christianized Filipinos in an American-era bahay in Parañaque. The Museo was followed closely by the Casa Manila house-museum in Intramuros, a reconstruction of an elite 1870s house. Since then, the revival of colonial architecture has returned high ceilings, large windows and sepia-toned interiors to Filipino homes. Authentic old elements now provide newly built houses with the patina of time. Traditional details resurface as functional items, connecting new architecture to the past.

Filipinos have learned to reuse antique building materials—wherever they can source them. The tropical hardwoods favored over other building materials by generations of Filipinos are lavishly used wherever possible. Old decorative details are creatively recycled within new spaces. Capiz windows, turned balusters, delicate wooden fretwork and structural elements from demolished houses find their way into the homes of Filipiniana-lovers. Hardwood lumber rescued from old houses is re-crafted into new floors, walls, and furniture. Wood varnished in various shades now tint the interiors of the house in the same subdued tones typical of the colonial house. The diffused light and muted wood tones are a flashback, placing the room in the same era as the ancestral sepia photographs that families pass down the generations.

Filipino homeowners have learned to recycle traditional ideas within new spaces. Continuing in the spirit of their ancestors who decorated Spanish colonial churches centuries ago, the bare walls, floors and ceilings in new houses are now embellished by contemporary Filipino artisans. Interiors are adorned with a mixture of textures, shapes, lines and colors that blur foregrounds into backgrounds. Antique furnishings are set as accents into a new house. Old carved double doors open one interior space into another. Sliding wooden windows with capiz shell set into the lattice, instead of glass panes, admit muted light. The polished warmth of flooring made from wide planks of recycled hardwood conjures an elegant ambience. Heritage, seen with new eyes, is now the starting point for a multitude of fresh designs.

One approach to adapting Filipino traditions takes its inspiration from nineteenth century upper-class families who lived genteel lives in houses that lined the streets of Intramuros. Their bahay na bato houses were built of the finest stone and the best hardwood. The interiors of their homes contained delicate carvings on heavy wooden doors and sophisticated collections of fine Filipino, Chinese and European furniture. Today the modern ilustrado attempts to recreate that elite colonial life in a new house that offers the urbane illusion of unlimited space; highlighted by traditional decorative art combined with contemporary pieces.

Another approach romanticizes the quaintly rustic or the downright folksy—what adherents sometimes call "jeepney-design" or a *Bahala-na* (leave it to fate) method in architectural design. Discarded materials, structural, architectural and decorative pieces from several demolished houses become the focal points or determinants for a new construction. Old pieces are recycled, sometimes force-fit to become new floors, doors, walls, windows and roofs. The result is a picturesque, hand-hewn house that makes light of the traditional *bahay*. The heritage of the past enriches the charm of the present, proving that the best design is timeless.

A church statue of San Miguel on horseback gallops through a recreated bahay na bato in Dr. Jaime Laya's basement. For years the Cultural Commissioner picked up "stray house parts" and eventually the pieces all fit together—"like a giant lego set"—into his modern Filipino home.

Ethnic and Elite

The master of this house of the late 1970s wanted his home to be horseshoe-shaped for good luck and the furniture to be modern— for peaceful dreams! Since then, Mr and Mrs Jose P. Cojuangco have lived successful lives in business, society, academe and politics. Mrs Cojuangco, a scholar of Muslim studies, is Governor of Tarlac Province. Her antiques are the house's centerpieces: especially the giant Moro pandis (wooden drums) from Mindanao and a choice selection of Batangas furniture. On the coffeetable she displays tribal arts from the Cordillera— conversation pieces for visitors. The raised dining room is all dressed in Muslim cloths and festive trimmings. The most unique cachet of this elite household is the antique hardwood floor—the 14-inch-wide boards bring the golden patina of age into a modern home.

Recreating Filipino Ambience

This house is an ordinary mid-1950s Manila house outside, but Dr. Jaime Laya's interiors have undergone numerous transformations to accommodate four children and a collection of Filipiniana. "The interiors are strictly homemade and have just evolved through the years, dictated by family possessions and collectibles—everything simply shifted around to make room for the new arrivals." The floor itself was a late arrival; all the narra floorboards came from (literally) house wreckers. That was the inexpensive way to fund a house. The habit of collecting Filipiniana became a lifestyle. Laya lives in a library (right) of books, paintings, and old architectural details that almost push the owner aside. An ornate archway marks the space; while capiz windows adapted from another house filter the light into his enlightened room. By the 1980s Laya recreated a complete stone-and-wood bahay under his main house (above). Adobe bricks, the large door of the basement and assorted woodwork came from Chinatown houses. Window grills and molave panels came from San Fernando, Pampanga.

A Provincial Manor

Inigo and Maricris Zobel insist that their home is just a basic, simple bahay kubo in Calatagan, Batangas. Businessman Inigo himself conceptualized the rustic abode as unpainted adobe brick walls around one large central room. The roof and ceiling are made of nipa woven with rattan vine and mangrove wood. The red Vigan tiles used for the flooring were stained with used motor oil to achieve an "antique look". To furnish his new/old home, Zobel sought out the scrounging king: "Boy" Vicente, a construction consultant adept at recycling discarded details from demolished houses. They combed the province sourcing old materials, being always "purist" and true to traditional Filipino homes. A magnificent carved door (main picture) became the entranceway amid a red brick door frame; the country bahay is built around two posts of beautiful old yakal wood found in a neighboring town.

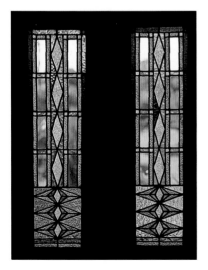

A Place in the Country

The Zobel couple fondly call their classy bahay kubo "Casa Molave", after the molave trees that used to surround the house. Today two old molave trees stand at the entrance to the lush, rolling property, and one giant slab forms their coffeetable among other rustic woods that are a running theme. The central living room comprises both antique wood accessories and new furniture made from old wood. The master bed, designed by Boy Vicente, is made from hardwood panels spliced together into a unique headboard and footboard. Outdoors, the garden on the hillside contains plants and materials from all over Batangas, including an antique door that is converted into the front gate to the yard. Nearby (left, top) is an authentic wood-and-thatch bahay kubo now painted in pastel shades, where the Zobel children live and play all weekend.

Principles of the Bahay

"It's a modern Filipino home that uses designs, concepts and elements from traditional homes, but interprets them according to the needs of a contemporary way of life". Dr. Nicanor Tiongson's house on a Quezon City hill is built of hand-me-downs: beams from the pre-war Quiapo Church; doors from the old Philippine General Hospital; colored glass from a Malolos relative's 1930s house; and furniture from demolished houses in Bulacan. Architect Rosario Encarnacion incorporated the owner's heritage into this unique house.

Right: The Spanish-inspired library contains a substantial Filipiniana collection, the owner being a scholar; "an obsessive Filipinologist."; and Artistic Director of the Cultural Center, who produced the CCP Encyclopedia of Philippine Art.

Left, above: Dr. Tiongson (seen in a sculpture by artist Julie Lluch) says this house was built around his personality and lifestyle. "The house is a second skin . . . The courtyard is the navel of the house, the sala is the face; the kitchen, the stomach; the bedroom and bathroom are organs of emission; the library is the head or brain; and the music room, the heart."

Left, below: Ventilation is achieved through high ceilings and open upper-wall passages between rooms. An inner courtyard and the high roof (with no ceiling) allows breezes to waft through the rooms. The house opens up to the tropical conditions wherever possible. The tower affords the breeze and a great sunset view.

Filipino Ethnic Haven

The furnishing and layout of this crowded house
is determined by the interests and profession of
social anthropologist David Baradas. Artifacts are
primarily from ethnic areas, with the occasional
nod to lowland mainstream tradition. There are no
foreign objects or artifacts in the house—"to give
full play to Philippine traditional art." Most items
have tales of tribal custom attached.
The calado panels—pierced wood dividers—under
the ceiling (above) are here lowland embroideries
on tribal-ethnic lines. The 43-inch-wide coffeetable
is a wooden container used for bread-making. On
the walls are a Tausog appliquéd tapestry;
handwoven hats; and handloom back-supports
from Jolo. Ifugao bulols (rice granary gods) guard
Baradas' ethnic haven.

Heritage Renovations

This houseproud attorney lived in a comfortable bungalow in Quezon City for years, until he decided on a change of style and environment—to create a Filipino-Spanish home reflective of his family's history and roots. The inspiration started with a carved arko or archway that fitted nicely over the dining alcove. He then ordered several capiz-shell light boxes to straddle the front door and line the transoms around the sala. Finally the urge to "go traditional" took over the flooring itself; he installed a beautiful floor of 12-inch tindalo planks—a wood that's harder than the narra. (Now he proudly invites friends over to go barefoot on his new floor!) The back-yard garden was designed by landscapist Shirley Sanders who reshaped a narrow space into a new entertainment area. She raised a high wall of adobe stone—"to complement the very Filipino interiors"; paved the ground with white stones; planted large ferns all the way up the back wall; and introduced a wide variety of vegetation in all corners.

An Artist's Space

Artist Claude Tayag's house in
Angeles, Pampanga, was recycled
from blessed old wood from a
demolished church—including a "nave"
that lets in light from above. Giant
Japanese strokes on his long white
closet complement the minimal array
of furniture, which he designed. His
big square room feels very modern,
very eclectic, very Tayag. Above: The
house resembles a beach bungalow
with a wide balcony and the pond
and riverstones below.

Left: A Chinese medicine cabinet
with 50 drawers is his mesa altar for
a big collection of small santos.

A Signature Space

Imagine his workers' consternation. His flooring was reconstituted, plank by plank, from the abandoned (lahar-ridden) bowling lanes of Bacolor. His bedroom doors were old panels given the once-over: Tayag subjected the most common wood-and-capiz elements to his painstaking method: the panels first were painted in thick layers of tropical colors and then scraped down—to achieve the faded, antique look! The traditional pillow rack or almario (main picture), meanwhile, holds woven abaca-covered throwpillows. Left: Outside Tayag's tiny but high-tech kitchenette (where he often demonstrates his prowess as Pampanga's finest culinary artist) stands an old-fashioned paminggalan, a slatted cabinet for storing plates. Above: Grillwork over frosted glass lines the room, alternating with persianas, slatted wooden jalousies that are adjusted by the center bar.

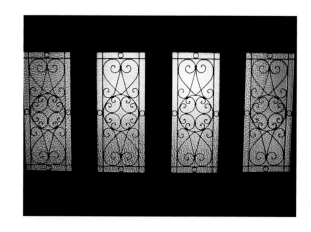

Native Context and Texture

Antique dealer Ricky Baylosis' creation is a
weekend retreat in Calatagan, Batangas, "with
wide open spaces; less walls for more ventilation
and a loft (instead of a proper bedroom) that opens
up to a verandah." He took five years to gather
the old materials and used lumber. The result is
an exquisite bahay textured with natural bamboo
wall-coverings and rattan furniture, hand-woven
tribal textiles, and sculptural artifacts from
the Cordilleras and Mindanao.

The Art of Creative Recycling

Mrs Alice Saldana fashions new houses from discarded materials. As the ultimate recycler, she claims, "It's all hit-or-miss! You have to gather the materials first, before even starting to plan a house". So she squirrels old wood away for a creative day. As in her bachelor son's house: The massive church door (right) was obtained first and the house built to fit it (just). An old ship's mast became the main pillar. Hardwood panels from a demolished mansion are reused in the floor. Ribs from a boat's hull are turned into window grills (above).

A Vigan Adaptation

This small (550 square meters) nineteenth century bahay na bato in Vigan has been adapted recently in the interests of livability. Jomar and Vicvic Villanueva are heritage-conscious: She's the "last in her line to save an old house in Vigan". He makes a living reproducing Vigan's "antique" furniture (above). When they adopted the ancestral bahay, they chose to adapt the roomy basement that used to be a zaguan or carriage area. It was a massive job: the ground was raised by 16 inches with poured cement and red Vigan tiles. The ceiling was lowered. Storage rooms were airconditioned so that they could serve as bedrooms—and the old house lives on.

Pearl Farm Resort

Pearl Farm Resort is a modern-ethnic confection in bamboo on Samal Island, an hour from Davao City. Built on the site of the original Aguinaldo Pearl Farm, the 11-hectare resort designed by architect Francisco Mañosa features three different designs of guest cottages, inspired by the shoreline architecture of the Samal, Mandaya and Maranaw tribes of Sulu. Coral walkways cross pools and form bridges, sampaguita-lined paths abound, a man-made waterfall provides music, and a three-tiered gazebo is there just for sea-gazers.

Left: The comfortable cottages display an array of Philippine hardwoods: flooring in yakal, posts and balconies of aged ipil-ipil, and stairs of molave. The furniture is stylish rattan-weave, usually seen only when it's exported.

153

Pearl Farm Villas

The six large bamboo villas on stilts
on nearby Malipano Island belong to
the Floirendo family members. Each
villa boasts an individual theme in
all-natural, all-tropical materials.
These attractive interiors are self-
decorated in Filipiniana style by
Margie Moran Floirendo, Miss

Universe 1973. The sala artifacts are mostly Muslim, from the Tausog saddle to the burial marker shaped like a horse. The bedrooms feature the lowland-provincial style with four-posters in narra. All traditional items are displayed with a sophisticate's flair.

Cafés on a Theme

Café Isabel (above) is housed in a 1927 American Victorian white house in San Juan, Manila. Opened up, terraced, and re-designed behind its original façade, the mansion today sports a "baroque-surfeit" look that whets the senses, even before one tastes Chef Gene Gonzalez's nouvelle fare. Right: The nineteenth century Crisologo family house has been transformed into the Aniceto Inn for visitors in the heritage town of Vigan, Ilocos Sur. Retaining its old ambience while adapting to

modern use, the new owners laid old red brick in repetitive arches, creating a café-nook that feels like a wine-cellar. The Café by the Ruins in Baguio City (main picture) began with the remaining single stone archway of the American Governor-General's mansion of the 1920s. In eight years, the artists behind the café have established their trendy venue amid the bamboo and pine wood. They also have a stylish cogon roof, carved posts and bamboo lamps and a dap-ay or Igorot meeting center beside the ruins.

Natural Influences

Augusto F. Villalon

*T*he connection between the rural Filipino home and nature is so close that its design and construction are dictated by its tropical enviroment. The wood, bamboo and palms growing in the immediate vicinity are the materials used to build the traditional house. The open area beneath the house is where the family gathers during the day, shaded from the hot sun but always in contact with the outdoors.

Today's gardens continue to reinforce the Filipino partiality for being outdoors and for keeping in close contact with nature. Landscaping receives much attention in the planning of modern Filipino homes. Patches of lawn stretch between masses of ornamental plants grouped around man-made slopes and mounds. Walks and pools of water meander through compositions of rock, pebbles, driftwood and waves of plants arranged into different settings, carefully coordinated to achieve the right mixture of colors, textures and shapes. The total scene, intended to appear as natural as possible, transforms nature into an overwhelming tropical wonderland. Nature, in all its glory, was never as lush, as romantic or as picturesque as this.

Modern Philippine gardens flow indoors, combining plants with any organic materials used to build or decorate the new house. In open terraces and covered porches, rustic floors of old stone and walls of weathered wood or recycled antique brick evoke the presence of nature. The Filipino house always provides an indoor area which allows the inhabitant to enjoy the outdoors. The modern Filipino house regards its garden as an alfresco living space.

In the rooms that bridge the indoors and outdoors, the shine of deep green foliage, dark polished stone, burnished hardwood and dull terracotta brick tie the colors of the interior to the earth. Large doors and windows bring unobstructed garden views into the house. Many new structures continue using wood, bamboo and thatch as principal building materials. Hand-crafted joinery reinterprets these materials into walls, ceilings and floors in an infinite variety of simple or elaborate patterns. Natural materials crafted in the best Filipino tradition produce comfortable, lightweight furniture. Chairs and tables combine hand-hammered wrought iron with wood, bamboo, rattan and hand-woven upholstery adapted from ethnic patterns. Canes and vines are woven into seats. If table tops are not of the finest tropical hardwood, then they are of marble, or of a mosaic of small tiles made from shells or stones. The natural materials used in construction and furnishing tie the new home to nature.

Houses that turn to nature for inspiration display a deep respect for the environment. Boulders and trees on the site are not disturbed. The new structures adjust and accommodate, rather than destroy, the organic elements existing on the site. Locations of old trees and the areas they shade determine the size and shape of terraces. Multi-level structures follow, rather than change, the natural land contours. Rock outcroppings are the natural walls of the interior areas constructed next to them. The ecologically sensitive house takes its cues from nature. It roots the home to the environment, continuing with the traditions of ecological harmony established long ago by the rural Philippine one-room house.

Natural materials are the traditional medium for Filipino craftsmanship. Inspired by natural forms, organic materials transform into sophisticated pieces of decorative art. Elegant floral motifs, vines and tendrils are carved into wooden objects or hand-embroidered on to fine textiles. Wooden fretwork delicately incised in elegant flowery patterns throws a lacework of shadows on house façades. Furniture is inlaid with tendrils and arabesques of shells. The creativity of the Filipino craftsman combined with the ease with which he adapts traditional ethnic, Oriental and Western design inspirations has led to an abundant repertoire of outstanding examples of decorative art. As the historical product of 400 years of Spanish rule followed by 50 years of American government, the Filipino is heir to a multicultural legacy.

Within the personalized environment of a Filipino home the old blends with the new, the natural with the synthetic, the traditional with the contemporary. This is an eclectic environment, a special enclave like no other. It is a living space where, even in the city, individuals live in touch with nature.

Filipino homeowners bring the environment indoors, combining lush greenery with weathered stones, wood and old Asian statuary. Couturier Chito Vijandre has designed his backyard to be as picturesque as his hand-crafted Italianate home.

Antipolo Garden Arts

Arts-patron Dr. Joven Cuanang encourages his artist-friends to design his home and garden in Antipolo to their hearts' content. His country house, renovated by architect Vicente Ampil, has a spacious Minimalist interior—what he calls the "Il-Mex" (Ilocano-Mexican) style— a single old red brick wall imported from Cuanang's northern hometown divides the space and exhibits some of his many modern paintings. Left: The bamboo bridge by the big rock waterfall leads to nowhere. Young artist Tony Leano applies zen principles to the environment, coaxing beautiful ideas from the lay of the land.

Previous page: An expansive moonlight deck amid the lush Antipolo vegetation. The artists constructed a bamboo meditation center, where they commune under the tamarind tree during the full moon.

Moonwalk Chapel

The Chapel of Mary Immaculate in Las Piñas—fondly called Moonwalk Chapel— is an interaction work by architect Francisco "Bobby" Mañosa and the late landscapist Rodney Cornejo. This "temporary" installation started when the congregation needed space and a neighboring landowner lent her land for an extension chapel—on the condition that nothing permanent be placed there and no trees be cut. Mañosa proposed the pitched tent concept, positioning a roof of wood and palm among the 14 live trees. Cornejo landscaped the interiors and fashioned the capiz doves circling down to the altar. Vines, netting and thatch give the space its organic texture. The worshipers' seats are log stumps—so naturally placed that Moonwalk Chapel feels like a campfire gathering.

Budji's Fantasy Garden

*A provincial homestead can be a joy
with a few inspirations from Budji
Layug—the designer who does wondrous
things with organic materials. His
bahay na bato in Pagsanjan, Laguna,
has all-stone quarters below and
all-wood rooms upstairs—full of old
Filipiniana and fine Laguna cooking.
The bahay has an outdoor staircase,
ascending without bannister to a
balcony from where one views the
garden with its gazebo of thatch
and natural poles atop brick columns.
Bordered with a fence of railway
ties—imbedded with stone grinders—
the garden holds Budji's collection of
horse figures in wood, stone and metal.
In the fishpond are his latest creations:
giant brass frogs and lizards; at porch
level, a wild brass orchid.*

A Tagaytay Condo

The challenge posed to designer-landscapist Roberto Borja was to express his client's love for old woods, rustic looks and Cordillera tribal artifacts in a compact condominium in Tagaytay. He does so by applying his own "love for nature" to the straight-edged space. Diffused lighting and casual anglings "open up" the boxy space. Natural tree-trunks "grow" from floor-to-ceiling and around corners. Old wood is used in the treatment of the ceiling and sitting areas, with irregular tree-trunks lined up as beams. Philippine tribal ikat-weaving figures in the upholstery and in the ceiling borders. The bedroom on the lower level features a four-poster bed made of polished hardwood tree trunks; with a mirror as a canopy and a wide sitting-bench board that doubles as a bedside table.

A Rustic Hideaway

Don Jaime Zobel wanted a "very small, very rustic and very Filipino house that would be a change of atmosphere from the sea to the mountain." A steep Mindoro slope became the dramatic site—with its breathtaking view of Puerto Galera below—and young Architect Noel Saratan had a free hand to design Zobel's dream. Saratan as idealist, artist and craftsman accomplished this his first solo creation using stone, bamboo, cogon—and much Japanese inspiration. Left: The circular staircase from the road to the entrance is an artwork in fine stone chips, spiraling—like a Cordillera dap-ay (meeting place)—to a zen garden in white sand. Right: The house stands on stilts and posts of poured concrete; but is completely "wrapped" with bamboo wicker and nito-weave panels (woven by Mindoro Island's Mangyan tribespeople, an adaptation of their traditional baskets). Right, first inset, is Saratan's tour de force entrance bridge: an imposing Japanese gateway made with bamboo, cogon and thick wooden pillars.

   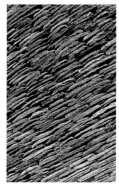

Marina del Nido, Palawan

A rustic resort for mariners in Bacuit Bay,
Palawan, Marina del Nido comprises just five
round-roofed, cogon-thatched huts with a
black granite cliff behind them and a long
white beachfront—amid one of the most
beautiful coastal areas in the country. The
Marina won a design award in 1996 for
its adaptation of materials (organic with a
conscience): "It was inspired by my study of
the architecture of indigenous Philippine tribal

groups for applications in contemporary use,
"says architect -manager Regina Lim.
Ms Lim confined her building materials to
quick-growing monocots such as bamboo,
cogon grass and anibong palm, lashed with
rattan vine. The largest pavilion is a thatched
open-air lounge with a peaked roof and
creative bamboo-and-paper chandeliers by
Baguio artist Perry Mamaril. A small
generator supplies Ms Lim's laptop—so
Marina del Nido doesn't feel totally isolated.

A Beach Longhouse

The specifications for this thatched house on a private slice of Puerto Galera beach were: To make it very Asian; to use all-local materials, such as bamboo, nipa and wood; and to make it very rustic, "although obviously very comfortable." Young architect Andy Locsin's design for Don Jaime Zobel's family resthouse—with his father's guiding spirit behind it—thus feels like an elegant Malay longhouse, comprising many rooms interconnected by open halls or walkways on stone-covered stilts. The insides of the thatched roof (right, top) are designed with rough-hewn crossbeams amid wide planes of fine bamboo textures. Right, below, the "very Filipino" walls of sliding capiz shell partitions and persianas (adjustable slatted windows) filter fascinating shadows and lights.

175

Elegance in Bamboo

The Zobels' front verandah is a family-
favorite setting in modern rattan. All the
interiors were decorated by Mrs Bea
Zobel, with advice from designer Johnny
Ramirez. The furnishings are from Cebu
City, native-design center of the South.
The girls' bedroom, shaded by wide
overhangs, is a showcase suite all
dressed in white.

176

Salakot House of Cebu

Owner Amparito Lhullier calls it the Salakot
House, as it looks just like a native hat (called a
salakot) atop its hill. This unique round confection
was designed in the 1970s by Lito Osmena,
Governor of Cebu and a builder with a creative
architectural bent. The thatched doughnut
house—both a recreation center and conversation
piece—is furnished with a 360-degree view of
Cebu, great sunsets and winds rushing through,
even from under the wide circular boardwalk.
Overhead, tree-branches leave no distinction
between structure and Osmena's nature-artistry.

Intriguing Isla Naburot

You feel like Robinson Crusoe the moment you step foot on to tiny Isla Naburot off Guimaras Island in the Visayas. Named after a tough climbing weed, Isla Naburot is the Saldana family's rustic private hideaway—that opened up to adventure-tourism about ten years ago. Read Rustic with a capital R: a pastiche of thatch and driftwood, shell bits and shipwreck art are ensconced around a white-sand beach and along the craggy coral rock that shelters it. The thatched village looks on to a shallow channel between the isles (the fishponds are opposite). The resourceful soul behind Isla is Dr. Alice Saldana, a practicing pathologist with an irrepressible creativity about her. In the 1970s she built six tiny houses for her children to stay in during vacations. As she collects old wood and loves to build, the rustic spaces were filled to her beach-combing heart's delight.

Island Adventure

Isla Naburot's most "adventurous"
accommodation faces the open sea.
Everywhere around, there's an
interesting orchestration of elements:
steep, sometimes precarious, climbs up
bamboo ladders or slippery planks
to huts atop coral outcrops or high amid
the jungle. As decoration, there are
crustaceans, shells, reptile skins and the
occasional whale bone. But there's
no electricity on Isla, just tiny candles or
kero-lamps to light your way to your
windy room at the top. An adventure-
stay on Isla is "not for everyone!"
manager Anne Saldana says. But
heaven comes with the home-grown Iloilo
hospitality—you get simply delicious
seafood fare, cooked over wood-fire stoves
and presented with aplomb, while sitting
next to the Saldana family, under
a canopy of a thousand stars.

183

Modern Filipino

Fernando Nakpil Zialcita

Modern architecture sought to strip buildings of all symbolic references to the past in order to concentrate on their basic structure and purpose. Postmodern architecture has reacted against this by relating the building once more to previous traditions, but, without being literal. While many Filipino architects professed to the Modernist creed in their office buildings, some connected with the past in their house designs. This is, after all, a country of year-long summers. Houses have to be cool and open, not everybody wants a fully airconditioned house. Moreover, a house has to look and feel like a home. The cultural memory of both architect and client subtly altered new house designs.

An interplay between tradition and modernity is manifest, for instance, in the work of Leandro Locsin, a Modernist architect by training. A son of Silay, a city famous for its turn-of-the-century houses, he grew up loving these houses for their graciousness and practicality. Their spirit suffuses his best works, modern though they be. The welcoming feel of the living room of his own residence in Forbes Park, Manila, owes much to this spirit. Though large to accommodate his many guests, it does not overwhelm the visitor. The scale is reduced by a narrow gallery of arches running between the living room and the exterior wall facing the garden. Instead of taking in the space of the room and wandering off immediately into the space without, the eye is invited to explore the enclosed living room, and at the same time to peer beyond: into the garden outside the arches, past the windows. The volada of old houses thus reappears, not in ornate tracery, but in a gallery of simple arches. Even his daringly constructed public buildings allude to the past. The Cultural Center of the Philippines and the Philippine International Convention Center may be large blocks of concrete, but they seem to float above the ground, for Locsin cantilevered the upper story outwards and emphasised its horizontality. It thus spreads quietly, parallel to the ground, and gently hovers above it, just like the upper story of the wood-and-stone house.

Filipino architects of the 1960s-1970s rediscovered the beauty and practicality of capiz shell in houses, whether for the city or the beach. It once seemed that the revered shellpane would disappear as an anachronism. Hovever, architects saw that these shellpanes created a mysterious light that softened the starkness of a modern room. Capiz has found new uses: as panels beside the main door for greater dignity, or as a long panel to frame part of a picture window. An admiration for Japanese esthetics, a hallmark of the modernist sensibility, took hold but was given a new twist. Shoji screens were reinvented by using shell paneled sliding doors. Interesting allusions surfaced, for sliding capiz windows of traditional Filipino houses may themselves have been influenced by Japanese carpenters working in seventeenth-century Manila. Meanwhile architects began using volcanic stone again because of its mottled texture, and blended this with wooden panels that were oil-finished to reveal the grain.

The naturalness of traditional, untrimmed, twisting houseposts reappears in contemporary beach houses and resorts. Sometimes the steep roof is of thatch with eaves that project more generously than in the farmer's hut. A modern innovation is to align the walls and partions on a curve. Together with the silent dance of the bent columns, this opens up the compact space of the rooms. Local traditions influence the more interesting designs.

Other architects, especially since the 1970s, have retained a fondness for the plain, untextured walls of contemporary architecture and for its no-nonsense look. Yet, despite themselves, their works are rediscoveries of tradition. Andy Locsin's design of an entrance hallway is a severely conceived, equally-sided, four-walled foyer. But it recalls the courtyard of nineteenth century Manila houses which also had a stairway, in a highly stylized manner, on one side of the patio. Roberto Quisumbing's living room looks extremely functional: untextured walls and a large glass window situated over a long rectangular door. Yet one senses the traceried panels of nineteenth century houses that opened up the walls to the light. Lor Calma's houses eschew ornate surface textures. Fitted into the plain, whitewashed walls are glass windows stretching from floor to ceiling, making his house seem like its nineteenth century ancestor: a birdcage.

Eclecticism arrives in Alabang, taking after New York in-vogue designer Saladino: unfinished cement walls mix with arty furnishings. A green Chinese door fronts the closet; the period chaise was found in a San Francisco thrift shop; the birdcage may be from Bangkok.

Indigenous Filipino Modern

*The Locsin house in Makati made waves in 1963
as a landmark in residential architecture. Designed
around the Philippine artifacts collected by
Architect Leandro Locsin, this was the first
modern home to fully incorporate indigenous
materials. The use of volcanic stone for entire walls
made the house a bridge between the nineteenth
century bahay and subsequent fashionable houses
in the city. The latticed arches in the living room
evoke, without literally copying, the nineteenth
century window gallery, called the volada.*

Filipino Modern

This vast glass gallery is the showplace home of Modernist architect Lor Calma: cool and geometric, allowing generous space for the sculptural arts and forms he loves. Architect Calma's interior design subtly recalls the principles of traditional Filipino houses: mostly windows, with limited walls, designed for letting in more light and air. The use of reinforced concrete, sleek metal frames and plate glass give these ideals a new look. And there is still a place for the traditional capiz shell in globe lights and doorways.

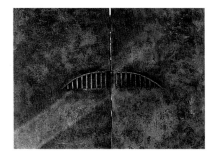

Contemporary Modern

Calma's details are fine and gestures bold. The architect fashions a comb on the gate (above) and a high modern waterfall drops into the swimming pool (below). The entrance (main picture) spells a dramatic transition from lush garden greenery into architect Calma's Minimalist gallery of modern art. Straddling the doorway, thin metal strips are interwoven in plaid patterns, thus softening the tropical light. While this is unmistakably a design of the 1980s-1990s in feeling, the ornament nonetheless recalls the Filipino penchant for framing window openings with capiz in grid formations.

Beach House and Tea House

Mindoro's "noble" beach house—conceptualized by Architect Leandro Locsin in 1972—is embedded into a mountainside overlooking the sea; and stands on stilts like the bahay kubo. Instead of outer walls, there are extra-wide roof overhangs over the posts (seen from bedroom, below). Natural tree trunks line the ceilings and perimeters; slatted floors surround the sala; and white coral is veneered on the walls. Just up the slope is the guest room, styled after a Japanese tea house—complete with shoji (now capiz!) screens.

Eclectic in Alabang

Ruby Diaz-Roa's residence is an eclectic garden-home in Alabang—graciously and harmoniously Asian in the living-dining areas; but chic and Manhattan-smart in the bedroom wing. Designed by Susan Castillo of Formoso Associates, the house has a languid layout in white coral stone, heeding the homeowner's wish "to continue her mother's romantic taste with

a beautiful lifestyle at all hours". Ms. Roa's select Asian artworks welcome one to her peaceful abode: a carved Hindu-Balinese temple door hangs on its side by an exquisite Philippine santo in prayer. The informal sala looks outward toward the garden, with rustic-native touches of vines woven around natural molave trunks and rattan sticks forming the ceiling texture.

Showcase of Filipiniana

Roberto Quisumbing salvaged his paternal ancestor's 1902 house—in order to remount it in his modern home 92 years later. His white-walled bungalow is a theater for remnants of the old house and for two antique collections: Filipiniana of Christians and Muslims; and tribal artifacts of the Cordillera highlands. Says the architect and plant-lover: "I tried to keep the house as simple and clean-lined as possible, so as not to compete with the collections." Main picture: The centerpiece of the new house remains his grandmother's old narra dining room. An archway of carved panels bears the same grapevine motif—signifying prosperity—as the one-piece narra table and armoire. The flowers are from the African tulip tree, gathered from Laguna.

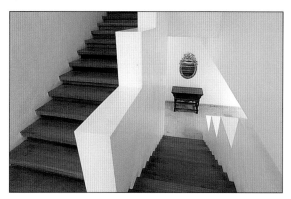

A Tribute to Barragán

Designing his first urban home, Architect Andy Locsin was "flexible" to the Latino-influenced ideas preferred by new homeowners Jaime Augusto and Lizzie Zobel. They all shared a mutual admiration for Luis Barragán, the Mexican architect who "cleaned" up the traditional hacienda. His bold, Modernist style was appropriate in the Philippine context, particularly in the stark foyer (main picture) that was originally meant to be a patio full of plants. Ms Zobel had noted and appreciated the form of the sculptural stairs and chose instead "to have a reflective pool and a very serene ambience that pays respect to the stairs. This is a homage to the central courtyard of old Spanish houses."

A Tribute to Spain

The Zobel house is Spanish-inspired in its use of red roof tiles but the owner is "reminded too of crowded Chinese compounds, where many roofs play against one another." The architect adapted the extra-thick walls of colonial architecture: a double layer insulates against the heat, so the three rooms below remain cool and refreshing. The most Filipino aspect of the house is the essential lanai or verandah on ground level; the very center of the residents' existence. Locsin made an expansive lanai—lined with a stately row of modern columns—and attached the formal rooms along its side. The breakfast room is bathed in fresh morning light, as it looks over the dark-tiled swimming pool.

A Glass and Bamboo House

An all-glass house that lives amid giant trees—this was the wild and "impossible dream" of a resource-ful artist couple in Antipolo. The couple took over the design, supervision and execution of the house—by experimentation. They decided that they would have no windows at all, just floor to ceiling glass walls surrounding a core of bamboo! This glass house is a brilliant sight by night, filled with light—a jewel-box, a wonder in the forest!

Paradise in Stone

This most unusual abode in the country is a freeform "pueblo" nestled into a slope of Tagaytay City, Cavite. This showplace home is the late Rafi Zulueta's tribute to Filipino creativity and engineering: a non-traditional pueblo-style house that he conceived in 1983. Constructed of poured cement and a "carpet" of stones, the Zulueta house is all curves. The form "flows" down the slope—like a long white cave—before it opens up to a two-level space with a giant skylight.

Pueblos in Tagaytay

Engineer Rafi Zulueta spent three long years realizing his vision and dream house in the Cavite highlands. The capacious interior features sinuous lines throughout and ceiling-to-floor plate-glass windows for viewing Taal Volcano's island-within-the-lake below. A pale stone-veneered dining table (above) harmonizes with the large organic space; while a freeform swimming pool (left) along the slope reflects the shape of Lake Taal below. The master bedroom (opposite, below) has wrap-around picture windows, so the resident can sleep in the wide embrace of the volcano view.

The Organic Country Club

Textured stone floors, giant rock gardens and contemporary rustic furniture have become interior designer Budji Layug's signature cast in stone. His appealing style is showcased in the elite and picturesque Tagaytay Highlands Country Club (above). Gnarled tree trunks are introduced as organic structures within the spacious, stone-carpeted atrium lounge. Furnishings are both chic and rustic with ethnic accessories.

Vernacular Filipino Modern

The bahay kubo is the native hut of the provinces, with pitched roof warding off the sun; hinged windows propped up by sticks; and stilts keeping the house high and dry. These are also the "vernacular" features echoed in architect Francisco Mañosa's contemporary Alabang home. Executed in modern materials such as stone, adobe, molave and narra, Mañosa's "Filipino House" has a high-pitched double roof that lets in the light and releases the heat of the day; and a wide porch protected by oversized roof eaves on long slanted poles. The spacious sala (right) has living, dining and entertainment areas adjoining—a space adjustable to one's needs. The master bedroom (left, top) has a private garden complete with graceful KuanYin.

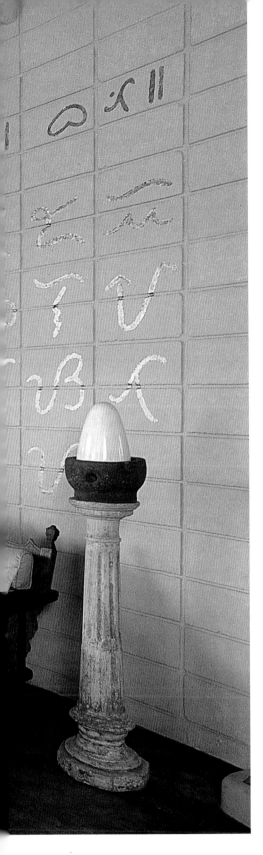

Filipino Post-Modern

This 1950s house in Laguna was an ordinary hollowblock house with a flat roof—until designer Ernest Santiago conjured it into unique Filipino chic. With paint and thatch, a feel for space and color, and an eclectic vocabulary, he designed a post-modern "traditional" Filipino house. The filigree cutwork usually found on window awnings now trims his eaves—in red lace!

Heaven in Laguna

Ernest Santiago has a way with natural materials. To an ordinary house he has added a circular thatched roof over the back terrace; a rustic nipa shed resting upon two classical cement columns. The ground was smoothly paved and stained "to simulate the sea". The terrace looks outward toward a bamboo grove and jackfruit tree. Nearby, stone grinder sculptures lead the way to his greatest joy—the lush and large tropical garden. When it rains, the view through the water cascading down those long nipa fronds is "heaven" in Ernest Santiago's Pagsanjan abode.

Amanpulo Resort

A Palawan afternoon provides guests with pristine turquoise seascapes and pure white sand beaches—seen from a private daybed outside a chic Amanpulo villa. Architect Francisco Mañosa has designed the exclusive Amanpulo Resort on Pamalikan, a 220-acre jewel of an isle in the Cuyo Group of Northern Palawan. Amanpulo is memorable for its unique privacy and luxurious accommodation in individual "casitas" (little houses).

Furniture Notebook

Rene Javellana

By the late seventeenth century Philippine artisans arrived at a synthesis of European-style furniture adapted to the tropical climate of the Philippine Archipelago and embellished with designs and motifs culled from the Orient. This marked a quantum leap in the development of Philippine furniture, a product of the cultural exchange between East and West. So pivotal is this period, that Filipino names for furniture types are almost always Spanish in origin; even the generic and popular name *muebles* cannot deny its Spanish roots.

Furniture and architecture go together. Prior to colonization, indigenous furniture was sparse. For the bamboo and thatch native house, the bahay kubo, heavy and bulky furniture was impractical. But the sturdy colonial bahay na bato supported by stout timbers could carry the weight of hardwood furniture. As more and more colonial buildings were erected, demand for furniture increased.

The first patrons of furniture were the Church and the State. The many churches and civic buildings had to be furnished. It is not surprising then that a simple long bench found in homes was patterned after the church pew and appropriately called *kapiya*, from the Spanish *capilla* or chapel. An adaptation of the kapiya, the *gallinera*, had a chicken cage built under the seat, popularly thought to be used for keeping fowl gathered by tax collectors in place of cash.

By the nineteenth century, furniture was being churned out in large quantities. Increasing wealth brought about by external trade stimulated the growth of a thriving furniture industry. Products of families of artisans and whole towns like Vigan, Ilocos Sur; Peñaranda, Nueva Ecija; Baliuag, Bulacan; Paete, Laguna; Bacolor, Pampanga; Malabon, Rizal; Iloilo, Cebu and Bohol in the Visayas were noted for their distinctive furniture. Two distinct regional styles emerged in Central and Southern Luzon, called by the cognoscenti "Batangas style" and "Baliuag style." The Batangas style of Taal and Lipa in the province of Batangas appeared in the seventeenth century. Chinese influence is clearly discernable in these pieces characterized by simplicity and grace, where form dominates over decoration. The Baliuag style is named after a town in Bulacan which specialized in bone-inlaid furniture.

The artisans, Filipino and Chinese, worked with a variety of tropical woods; close grained and dense, they responded well to polishing and varnishing. Furniture came in various earth shades: blood-red from tindalo or balayong wood; reddish brown from narra also called Philippine mahogany; yellowish from molave, a wood similar to teak; even alternating bands of black and brown from kamagong or bands of black and brownish green from iron wood, similar to ebony. These were finished by polishing and waxing or applying a clear varnish. On softer woods or woods of lower quality, a heavy black or dark brown stain and varnish was thickly applied to hide the imperfections of the wood.

As foreign ships called on Manila bringing with them European models, furniture styles evolved further. In the nineteenth century revivalist architecture and art were the vogue. From this period emerges what is called locally Luis Quince, a style of furniture whose affinity with the French prototype is the use of cabriole legs. Victorian horsehair stuffed sofas became the model for the graceful mariposa chair characterized by its butterfly-like back. Later, neogothic motifs emerged. Furniture from this period can be called classical, not because it shows a marked Graeco-Roman touch, but because this furniture provides the touchstone for later developments. The easy assimilation of foreign styles became a tried and tested formula so that during the next century Art Nouveau- and Art Deco-inspired furniture, made of hardwood became all the rage. The generous use of natural materials persisted into the post World War II period, where the clean lines of Scandinavian furniture, of Chinese Ming, and of designers such as Mies van der Rohe, Marcel Breuer, Eero Saarinen and Harry Bertoia served as models. But above all the skill of the experienced Filipino artisan, first proven during colonial times, has proved to be the lynchpin of all developments in Philippine fine furniture.

Lounging through the lazy afternoon on cane-woven butacas at the Casa Manila in Intramuros. New furniture appeared in the seventeenth century—the Europeans brought over their styles and Chinese and native craftsmen reworked these models into a cool island style.

Traditional Bedside Manners

Aparador de Tres Lunas.
Picturesquely described as a wardrobe
of three moons, relating
to the three mirrors attached
to its doors, this unusually
spacious wardrobe was made
for the master bedroom.
Casa Manila collection

Mesa altar. This classic altar table
from Baliaug, Batangas, is made of
tindalo, inlaid with dark kamagong
and bone. The characteristic
ornamentation is a diamond
and cat's eyes pattern.
Paulino Que collection

Comoda. This exquisite chest
of drawers is made of fine-grained
kamagong with silver fittings. One of
a pair, it is dated to the early nineteenth
century. Provenance: Manila.
Paulino Que collection

Painadora. Ladies' dresser with drawers and windows; the more elaborate version, the tremor, had three adjustable full-length mirrors. Casa Manila collection

Comoda. This ornate chest of drawers is inlaid with both bone and mahogany wood, indicating its origins in Pampanga, where they like their drawers decorative. D.M. Guevara collection

Kuna. Patterned after a turn-of-the-century European brass crib, this hardwood baby crib has lathe turned-spiral posts and stretchers. D.M. Guevara collection

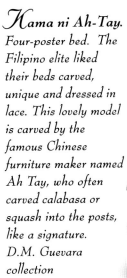

Kama ni Ah-Tay. Four-poster bed. The Filipino elite liked their beds carved, unique and dressed in lace. This lovely model is carved by the famous Chinese furniture maker named Ah Tay, who often carved calabasa or squash into the posts, like a signature. D.M. Guevara collection

The Protocol of Chairs

Diban. *Built to serve as lounging chair and day bed, the diban's graceful curves, caned seat, back and arm rests speak of leisurely afternoon naps, a respite from the tropic heat. Provenance: Laguna. D.M. Guevara collection*

Window or Procession High Chair. *Usually placed beside a window in the living room, this high chair was made for watching the passing street scene, especially religious processions. Provenance: Ilocos. D.M. Guevara collection*

Art Nouveau Love-Seat. *Built for a couple plus a chaperone, this seat uses Art Nouveau motifs, which were in vogue in the early twentieth century. D.M. Guevara collection*

Silya. *Armchair with arm rests ending in graceful spirals. Provenance: Bulacan. H.J. Springer collection*

Silla Perezosa. *A variation of the butaca, the silla perezosa or lazy chair is characterized by flat and extended arm rests and reclined back, built for short naps and leisure. Paulino Que collection*

Mariposa. *This hardwood and cane sofa, named after its graceful butterfly-shaped back, is adapted from the Victorian horsehair sofa. D.M. Guevara collection*

Sheraton-inspired Bulacan armchair. *British trading houses flourished in nineteenth-century Manila, bringing English taste to the Philippines, such as the clean lines of this chair. H. J. Springer collection*

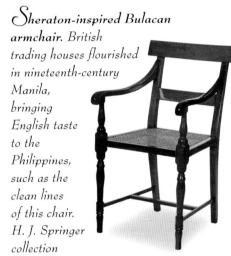

Silya. *This rustic armchair from Batangas emphasizes utility and simplicity. H. J. Springer collection*

Vienna furniture. *In 1851, Austrian Michel Thonet exhibited his knockdown steam-bent birch furniture at the Crystal Palace in London. His chairs were exported to the Philippines, where they were copied and adapted using hardwood. A variety of chairs, sofas, and rockers were made in the Philippines. D.M. Guevara collection*

221

The Hospitality Habit

Capiya. Inspired by the church pew, this long bench was made for tenants waiting for their turn to make a call on the landlord. The unusual length of this bench made an extra pair of legs necessary at midpoint. Casa Manila collection

Bastonera. A relic of more genteel times, the hat and cane rack was placed at the caida or foyer of a house for gentlemen to hang their hats and canes and for ladies to leave their parasols. D.M. Guevara collection

Lamesa. The name indicates the dining table's foreign pedigree. Made of hardwood, this six-seater dining table with marble top was probably made for a mezzanine apartment or entresuelo, built in urban houses for guests or offices. Casa Manila collection

Escritoryo. Made for an office, this desk or writing table has a double flip top so that business partners could work facing each other. Casa Manila collection

Silya. This chair from Bulacan has adapted elements from Sheraton furniture. D.M. Guevara collection

Daybed and capiz divider. Built for lounging or for short naps, this daybed has a headrest on either end. The divider gave some privacy or divided large spaces. Made of wood and translucent capiz shells, the divider allowed light to fill interiors. Provenance: Ilocos. Quema collection

Butaca. The lounging chair with cane back and seat was a comfortable piece of furniture for a tropical climate. D.M. Guevara collection

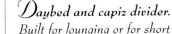

Vajilera. Fine crystal, porcelain plates and silverware were needed for the elegant table. When not in use, they were displayed in crystal cabinets with glass panels. Casa Manila collection

Mesa altar. This table was generally used as a family altar, however it was used for storing silverware and linen. Characteristics of the mesa altar are drawers beneath the table top and the stretchers that reinforce the legs. Casa Manila collection

Baul. Imitating the tooled leather covers of Spanish sea chests, these seventeenth-century narra-wood chests were used for long-term storage. Paulino Que collection

Lamesa. Refectory table. This fine seventeenth century heirloom in tindalo wood came from a church, but has been used for other things, including the buffet in a dining room. This Pampanga-made table has Chinese-influenced ball and claw feet. Paulino Que collection

Mesa Altar. This carved altar table made of reddish tindalo and dark kamagong wood has fine Rococo-style ornamentation. Provenance: Batangas, eighteenth century. Paulino Que collection

Sillon or Butaca. Lounging chairs with extended arms in narra and kamagong. Provenance: Quezon, Southern Luzon, early nineteenth century. Paulino Que collection

Silya. *A pair of sturdy armchairs in Philippine narra and rattan cane-weave. Provenance: Central Luzon, eighteenth century.*
Paulino Que collection

Sungkaan. *The Chinese shell-drop game found its way to the Philippines. This receptacle from Batangas was carved from one piece of wood.*
D.M. Guevara collection

Aparador. *A generic name for cabinets. The term is generally used for a wardrobe, with a mirror attached on the door. This dark beauty is from Pampanga, made of heavy kamagong wood.*
D.M. Guevara collection

Mesa altar. *Ornate altar table. The name suggests that this was used as a family altar; it was also a buffet table for a dining room. Provenance: Leyte, Visayas, eighteenth century.*
Paulino Que collection

Comoda. A chest of drawers kept everything: clothes, candles, jewelry. This piece has many secret compartments; the cabinet top opens to reveal a drawer for keeping land titles and the two columns can be opened to reveal a compartment for jewelry.

This piece made of kamagong is inlaid with animal bone and belongs to the Baliuag style. Oral reports indicate that this chest was made for an exhibition in Europe during the third quarter of the 1800s. *Paulino Que collection*

Escritoryo. This desk has a drop-leaf writing table supported by retracting supports. The drop-leaf hides small compartments for paper, pens, and other writing supplies. *Paulino Que collection*

Silya. This small armchair from Batangas has a wide arm shaped as a graceful volute. *Paulino Que collection*

Capiya. *This popular version of the church pew was made for country use. The unusual length of this bench from Batangas indicates it may have been made for the home of a wealthy landlord.*
D.M. Guevara collection

Occasional Table.
Round tables such as these were placed in a house's foyer or caida or used as side tables near beds.
Paulino Que collection

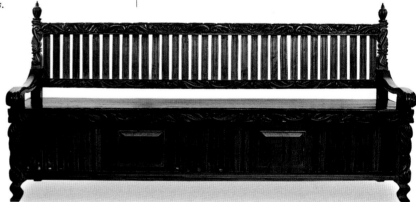

Gallinera. *This adaptation of the capiya bench had a chicken cage built under the seat for keeping the fowl gathered by tax collectors in place of cash.*
D.M. Guevara collection

Lamesa. *A Hepplewhite-inspired table of dark kamagong wood made for a banquet. Six legs support the length of the table.*
Paulino Que collection

Philippine Folk Provincial

Silya. Bamboo chairs with woven backs and seats such as these are common in China. This chair of uncertain provenance may have been imported or may have been copied from Chinese models.
D.M. Guevara collection

Silya. This rustic rocking chair made from mangrove branches (which sets it apart from other country chairs) is meant to be brought outdoors occasionally or left on a verandah.
D.M.Guevara collection

Almario. The Spanish almario was a cabinet made to display weapons. But the Philippine almario was made for more peaceful purposes. Built in various sizes, this four-legged, open bedroom piece stored pillows, mats and linens during the day.
D.M.Guevara collection

Bamboo table. This close-weave bamboo table with fish designs burnt into the smooth surfaces is a rare piece done by the artisan Nicolas Badua of Ilocos.
D.M. Guevara collection

Paminggalan. Plate-cabinet. The name suggests that this piece of furniture has pre-colonial roots. From the local word *pinggan,* plate, this slatted and airy cabinet was used to store plates and left-over food. Rustic versions were made of bamboo. *Casa Manila collection*

Dulang. The traditional Filipino dining table was very low (to sit by on the floor), rectangular or round. This dulang made of tindalo wood is unusual for its length. *Paulino Que collection*

Baul. This rustic bamboo chest sourced outside Manila may have once held papers and sundry stuff on a short-term basis. *D.M. Guevara collection*

Index

page numbers in **bold** indicate illustration

VISUAL INDEX
Locations of houses featured

Photography Credits

Luca Invernizzi Tettoni:
back cover; pages 20; 24; 25; 26; 27; 28 (*top right*); 30-31; 32-33 (*all images*); 35 (*main picture*); 36-37; 38 (*top right*); 39 ; 40-41; 42-43; 44-45; 48; 54; 55; 56; 57; 65 (*top*); 66; 67; 68; 69; 76-77, 77; 78; 79; 80-81; 81; 82; 82-83; 84-85; 85; 86; 87; 88-89; 89; 90; 91; 92; 102 (*top left*); 118; 119; 120; 120-121; 122; 122-123; 124; 124-125; 140; 141; 148; 148-149; 166-167; 167; 168; 168-169; 170; 171; 172; 173; 174; 175; 176; 176-177; 178; 178-179; 180; 181; 182-183; 183; 186-187; 187; 192-193; 193; 198-199; 199; 200; 200-201; 204; 204-205; 206; 207; 210-211; 211; 212-213; 213; 214-215; 215.

Tara Sosrowardoyo:
front cover; pages 4-5; 5; 6-7; 8-9; 10; 13; 16; 17; 22; 23; 28 (*inset, main picture, top left*); 29; 38 (*main picture, top left and middle*); 46; 49; 50; 51; 52; 53; 58-59; 60; 60-61; 62; 63; 64; 65 (*bottom*); 70; 71; 72; 72-73; 74; 96-97; 98; 98-99; 94; 75; 100; 100-101; 106; 107; 110; 111; 112; 113; 114; 115; 116; 117; 126; 128-129; 130; 131; 132; 133; 134; 135; 136; 137; 138; 139-139; 142; 143; 144; 144-145; 146; 147; 150; 151; 152-153; 153; 154; 155; 156; 157; 158; 160-161; 162; 163; 164; 164-165; 184; 188; 189; 190; 190-191; 194; 195; 196-197; 197; 202-203; 203; 208; 209; 223 (*top left, bottom left*).

Emil Davocol:
pages 34-35 (*all images except main picture*); 95; 103; 102 (*middle and bottom*); 108; 216; 218 (*bottom left*); 219; 220; 221; 222; 223 (*top right, middle, bottom right*); 225 (*middle, right*); 227 (*top, middle right*); 228; 229 (*bottom left, bottom right*).

Dick Baldovino:
pages 218 (*top, bottom right*); 224; 225 (*top left, bottom left*); 226; 227 (*middle left, bottom*); 29 (*top*).

Quincy Castillo:
pages 104; 104-105.

Ben Razon:
page 109.

Photographs on pages 14 and 15 courtesy of **John Silva**

Photograph on page 12 courtesy of **Jonathan Best**

Map artwork: **Anuar Abdul Rahim**

Acknowledgements

in alphabetical order

THE PROJECT STAFF
Henrietta Bolinao, *Public Relations Consultant*
Mylah M. Cornista, *Coordinator*
R. Agus "Rechy" Rachim, *Photo Assistant*
V. Alec Reyes, *Photo Assistant*

EDITORIAL CONSULTANTS
David B. Baradas, *Anthropologist*
Dr. Jaime Laya, *Cultural Commissioner*
Ms. Doris Magsaysay Ho, *Civic Leader*
Augusto F. Villalon, *Architect*
Ramon N. Villegas, *Historical Researcher*
Ramon R. Zaragoza, *Restoration Architect*
Special thanks go to Fernando Nakpil Zialcita
for overall guidance regarding Filipino history
and culture; and invaluable assistance in reviewing
the captions.

GUIDES AND HELPERS
Manila
Vic Gloria
Ingrid Guerrero, Gabby and Fermin, *Magsaysay Lines*
Mrs Joan Hubbard, *US Embassy*
Ricky Jaro, *Nissan Rent-a-Car*
Hans Juergen Springer
Irene Tan, *Mosaique Communications*
Annie de Leon, *Philippine Airlines*
Gerry Respeto
Annie Ringor, *Manila Hotel*
Joe Salazar
Monique Trinidad, *New World Hotel*
Willie Verzosa, *Likha Antiques*

Laoag and Vigan, Ilocos
Abe, *Town Auto Supply*
Louie Acosta, *City Guide*
Jomar Villanueva

Baguio City, Cordillera
Becky, *Café by the Ruins*
Fred Guimtaya, *US Embassy*
Tommy Hafalla, *Photographer*
Diana Negroponte, *US Embassy*

Pundaquit, Zambales
Coke Bolipata, *Pundaquit Cultural Center*
Doris Magsaysay Ho
Randy, *driver, Vital Car*

Angeles and San Fernando, Pampanga
Dona Carmen Lazatin
Dr. Jojo Valencia, *City Guide*
Michael Weiss, *General Manager, Holiday Inn Resort*

Malolos, San Miguel, Bulacan
Dez Bautista, *City Guide*

El Nido, Palawan
Gina Lim, *Manager, Marina del Nido*
Romelynne, *Airport Manager, Air Soriano*

Bacolod, Negros Occidental
Ernest Baker, *Casa Grande Antiques*
Esperanza and Marina, *Montilla-Tomkins hacienda (Ubay)*
Ruska Gamboa, *Silay Heritage Foundation*
Ella Gonzaga, *Lizares mansion, Talisay*
Ramon Hofilena, *Silay Heritage Foundation*
Mang Ray and Emma, *Lizares mansion, Talisay*
Vinton, *driver, Far Go*

Cebu City, Cebu
Faye Contemplo, *Alegre Beach Resort*
Tony Flores, *Director, Casa Gorordo*
Amparito Lhullier
Charles Muertegui, *City Guide*
Vincent, *driver, Autocorp*

Iloilo
Ben, *driver, Buddleia*
Saffy Ledesma II, *City Guide*
Rafael and Mariflor Lopez-Vito
Anna, Alice, Isa and Pons Saldana, *Isla Naburot*

Tagaytay, Cavite
Noel Benitez, *Taal Vista Hotel*
Nick Celdran, *Tagaytay Highlands Country Club*

Taal, Batangas
Dindo Montenegro, *City Guide*

Puerto Galera, Mindoro
Gerry Lane
Andy Locsin, *Architect*
Don Jaime Zobel, *Chairman, Ayala Corporation*

Pamilikan Island, Cuyo, Palawan
Pierre Baumgartner, *Amanpulo Resort*

Davao
Linda Lagdameo, *Pearl Farm Resort*
Margie Moran Floirendo

Artifacts Collections
David B. Baradas, *private collector (kitchen implements)*
Dominador Ferrer Jr., *Intramuros Administration*
Richard Lopez, *private collector (silver and piña)*
Bernie Manansala-Raphael, *Nayong Pilipino*
Nori Mapa, *Nayong Pilipino*
Tony Martino, *Via Antica (santos, ivories)*
Jojo Mata, *Intramuros Administration*
Paulino Que, *(furniture)*
Ramon Villegas, *Katutubo Artifacts & Crafts (silver, embroidery, ivory heads)*
Ramon R. Zaragoza, *private collector (handwoven textiles)*

THE FURNITURE COLLECTIONS
D. M. Guevara collection
The collection is officially called the *Museo ng Buhay Pilipino* collection of the D. M. Guevara Foundation, Inc. First assembled in 1975, the collection was originally a house-museum called *Museo ng Buhay Pilipino* (Museum of Philippine Life) and it concentrated on the traditional folk furniture of the lowland Christian majority. The MBP collection was donated to the Nayong Pilipino theme park in 1993 and is now on display at the Bulacan-style *Bahay na Tisa*.

Paulino Que collection
This private collector focused on classic Filipino furniture in the early 1980s. His collection is dedicated to preserving the very finest pieces of the eighteenth and nineteenth centuries. Photographs of selected pieces of furniture were taken by Dick Baldovino and have been generously lent to *Filipino Style*.

Casa Manila collection
The Intramuros Administration started to collect furniture from 1980 onwards for the purpose of furnishing the Casa Manila Museum with a permanent exhibition. The collection focuses on eighteenth and nineteenth century Spanish colonial furniture and other pieces dating from the colonial period. The largest pieces photographed for *Filipino Style* belong to the Casa Manila collection.

Thanks are due to the following companies for their generous support of this project.

New World Hotel, Makati
Holiday Inn Resort, Clark Field
Taal Vista Hotel, Tagaytay
Pearl Farm Resort, Davao
Cebu Plaza Hotel, Cebu
Alegre Beach Resort, Cebu
Marina del Nido Resort, El Nido
Isla Naburot, Iloilo
Amanpulo Resort, Cuyo
Air Soriano
Universal Motors Corporation